P9-EED-848

Grammar and Meaning

An Introduction for Primary Teachers

Louise Droga · Sally Humphrey

TARGET TEXTS

Copyright © Louise Droga and Sally Humphrey 2003

Published and distributed by

Target Texts
PO Box 359
Berry NSW 2535
AUSTRALIA

National Library of Australia Cataloguing-in-Publication data:
Droga, Louise.
Grammar and meaning : an introduction for primary teachers.
ISBN 0 9580440 1 5.
1. English language - Grammar - Study and teaching (Primary).
I. Humphrey, Sally. II. Title.

372.61

Cover and text design by Andrew Burns
Printed by Southwood Press Pty Limited
76-82 Chapel Street Marrickville NSW 2204 Australia

Disclaimer
The opinions expressed in the example texts in this book are not necessarily those of the publisher or authors.

THIS BOOK IS DEDICATED TO

THE MANY TEACHERS AND STUDENTS

WHO SHARE OUR LOVE OF LANGUAGE AND LEARNING

Acknowledgements

We would like to express our thanks to the following people for their invaluable feedback and editorial comments on various chapters of this book:

Sue Bremner (Curriculum Directorate, NSW Department of Education and Training)

Jon Callow (University of Western Sydney, Bankstown)

Brian Dare (Lexis Education, Adelaide)

Pauline Jones (Charles Sturt University, Bathurst)

Lesley Ljungdahl (University of Technology, Sydney)

Lorraine McDonald (Australian Catholic University, Sydney)

Anne Thwaite (Edith Cowan University, Perth)

Katina Zammit (University of Western Sydney, Bankstown)

Thanks must also go to Andrew Burns for his tireless efforts with layout and design and for yet another great cover!

To our respective husbands, Ian and Edward, we thank you yet again for your endless patience and support throughout this project. To our children, Emily, Jenny, Christopher and Rosemary, and their friends for allowing us to raid their portfolios for texts and to Ley Wighton and her Year 5 Wilkins Public School class for great ideas.

We would also like to thank the Primary English Teaching Association for granting us permission to reproduce copyright material from Beverly Derewianka's *A Grammar Companion for Primary Teachers* (1998).

Contents

1 A social view of language

In this chapter, we give a brief introduction to the view of language that underpins this book—a view that is concerned primarily with how we use language to make meaning. This is a social view of language. It is based on theories from sociology and linguistics, especially contributions from systemic functional linguistics (Halliday 1994; Halliday & Hasan 1976; Martin 1993; 2003).

The book is based on the assumptions that:

1. Language is functional

One of the fundamental assumptions in this book is that language is *functional* —it enables us to get things done. We use both spoken and written texts to achieve different goals or social purposes. Texts that share the same social purpose and have many of the same features are called genres or text types.

The notion of function relates not only to text, but to the language itself. The language we use in different spoken and written text types serves a number of functions simultaneously. Halliday describes these functions as :

- The experiential function—the way we use language to represent our experience of the world

- The interpersonal function—the way we use language to interact with others

- The textual function—the way we use language to create well organised and cohesive texts, both spoken and written.

The words we choose and the way we organise them within texts reflect these functions and help the text achieve its purpose.

2. Language is a resource for making meaning

The different functions of language relate to particular areas of the language system. The language system is a network of grammatical and lexical choices which can be seen as a 'tool-box' or *resource* for making meaning.

We use different lexical and grammatical resources from this toolbox to make or represent the different kinds of meaning. In other words, we draw upon the different areas of the language system depending on whether we are representing:

- what's going on, who's involved and the surrounding circumstances (ie. experiential meanings)

- the roles, relationships, and feelings involved in interacting with others (ie. interpersonal meanings)
- the different modes and channels of communication (ie. textual meanings).

3. Language is influenced by the context of use

The texts we use and the meanings we make with language are influenced by a number of factors outside language—those associated with the context in which language is being used. Features of the 'context' which may influence and shape our language use include:

The cultural context

This refers not only to the broad cultural practices associated with different countries or ethnic groups but also to the institutionalised practices within groups such as schools, sporting associations or Internet chat groups. These cultural practices shape the way we achieve goals through language (ie. the text type). For example, in the school context, there are many text types serving purposes associated with playing, administration and regulating behaviour as well as learning.

The socio-cultural context

Language also varies according to the different orientations or backgrounds of the groups within cultures. Sociologists and linguists have noted, for example, that factors such as socio-economic status, gender, ethnic background and age have a great influence on language choices.

The specific context

Aspects of the specific or local context also have a great influence on language. These include, for example, the activity we are engaged in, the nature of the interaction and the channel of communication. In the school context, important influences include the specialised activities within different curriculum areas, the different roles of teacher or student and the variety of modes used for learning (eg. textbooks, web-pages or spoken text).

Types of learning

The different types of learning that occur within and beyond schooling also influence our language use. Some learning will involve developing the specialised knowledge and understandings which are considered important within different cultures. Some learning will involve challenging and critiquing the assumptions on which this knowledge is based. And importantly, other learning involves transforming and 'renovating' knowledge in order to bring about social action and change.

Implications of a social view of language for teaching and learning

The social view of language described above has important implications for teaching and learning language in the primary school and beyond.

Firstly, understandings about language are important for learning in all curriculum areas, not just English. Language varies in different subjects. For example, the language of maths is different in many respects to the language of history. Therefore, teachers and students need to be familiar with the specialised uses of language associated with each area of the curriculum.

We also need to acknowledge that as students move through the primary school, the role of written language becomes increasingly important. As students engage with more specialised subject area learning, they need to access and demonstrate knowledge and understandings via written text types with increasing complexity.

Another important implication is that the development of students' language does not take place 'naturally'. Rather, it occurs in social contexts, usually those of schooling and other educational institutions, in interaction with language aware teachers.

Finally, a social view of language provides a language for talking about language —a metalanguage. This makes it possible for teachers to be explicit about functional aspects of language when modelling and jointly constructing texts with students. In addition, it allows teachers and students to describe and critique the resources used by writers and speakers to construct different versions of reality in the texts they produce.

Exercise 1.1

Your own primary English syllabus (or equivalent) should contain a rationale which describes the view of language upon which the document is based. Read this carefully and then consider the questions below.

i. Does the document identify the view of language upon which it is based?

ii. How would you describe this?

iii. Does the document list any broad aims and objectives? What are they?

iv. How does the document describe the role of language in learning?

v. How does the document address language development?

Exercise 1.2

At the end of each chapter, you will be asked to build a 'glossary' of the key terms used in the book. Use the following table to begin your glossary, by recording your understandings of some of the specialised terms introduced in this chapter.

Term	Your understanding of the term
Genres	
Experiential function	
Interpersonal function	
Textual function	
Cultural context	
Socio-cultural context	
Specific context	
Metalanguage	

2 Text types: a context for exploring grammar

The different texts that students are required to interpret and produce at school provide a useful starting point for looking at patterns of grammar and meaning. In this chapter we introduce some of the text types that are important for learning in the primary school and further explore the relationship between text and context by looking at:

- The social purpose and structure of different text types

- The role of different text types in learning across the school curriculum.

Although not a major focus, this introduction will help establish a context for the more detailed explorations of grammar in subsequent chapters.

2.1 Text types and social purpose

In Chapter 1 we saw that the way we get things done in our culture using language is through different text types or *genres*. We use a particular text type depending on our social purpose. This will vary according to the context within which we are using language—the home, the local community, the workplace, the school etc. There are text types which inform, entertain, argue a point, order meals, complain about services and achieve many other goals.

Exercise 2.1

The following segments of text are taken from text types encountered by one person over a week as they went about their daily life. Read through the segments and try to predict some aspects of the context of each segment. Use the questions on Table 2.1 to guide you. A response to the first segment has been provided.

Table 2.1

Questions / Text Segments	What is the social purpose of the text?	Is the segment taken from the beginning, middle or end of the text? How do you know?
Segment 1.1 OK, well turn on the oven first	To instruct someone how to do something.	Beginning—I know that when cooking you generally turn on the oven to start with so that it's at the right temperature.
Segment 1.2 In conclusion, bikes should only be ridden on the footpath.		

(continued)

Questions / Text Segments	What is the social purpose of the text?	Is the segment taken from the beginning, middle or end of the text? How do you know?
Segment 1.3 Once upon a time ...		
Segment 1.4 After we visited the museum, we returned to school.		
Segment 1.5 The tallest hardwood tree in the world is the mountain ash.		
Segment 1.6 This leads to soil erosion.		

As Exercise 2.1 demonstrates, text types occur in order to achieve a goal or social purpose. In order to achieve its purpose a text type has a particular structure, with parts or *stages* which are clearly recognisable. Here is an example of a simple fairy story, or more technically, a narrative. It has been annotated to show its typical structure.

Text 2.1: Narrative

Social Purpose: To entertain and instruct through dealing with unusual and unexpected development of events.

Text structure

Orientation	Once upon a time in the middle of the forest, there lived a girl named Jane with her father, a poor woodcutter.
Complication with Evaluation	One day, the little girl's father did not come home from the forest and Jane became more and more frightened that he had had an accident. She didn't know what to do because she was very afraid of the dark.
Resolution	Finally she plucked up all her courage and headed out to the clearing where she thought her father had been that day. After two long hours searching, she finally found him. His foot had been trapped under a log and he couldn't lift it himself. Jane helped her father to free himself and they went home happily.
Coda (optional stage which evaluates events)	Jane was very glad she had not been too frightened to go in search of her father.

Some text types (eg. traditional narratives like Text 2.1) are more fixed and predictable in structure than others because of the relative lack of change in the purposes they were created to achieve. However, for the most part text types are dynamic and change over time as the purposes they were established to achieve change. Text types are also intricately related to the culture in which they are created. This understanding of culture relates not only to ethnicity or country but also to particular groups people belong to (eg. university students or religious groups).

2.2 Text types and their structure

One of the differences between text types is that they have different structures. This is because the parts (or *stages*) of the text work to achieve the particular purpose for which it is written. Texts 2.2 and Text 2.3 have been written to achieve different purposes. The stages of each text have been labelled to show their function.

Text 2.2: Explanation

Social Purpose: To explain scientifically how technological and natural phenomena come into being.

Text Structure	Why Volcanic eruptions occur
Statement of phenomenon	Volcanic eruptions often occur at the boundaries of two colliding of plates. These plate boundaries are called subduction zones.
Explanation sequence (related according to time and cause)	When the two plates collide, one plate is forced underneath the other. Because the plate moves downwards, it heats up. This heating creates magma. As the heat and pressure continue to build up, the magma bursts through the crust. This results in hot lava and gases being released into the atmosphere along with rocks and smoke.

Text 2.3: Review

Social Purpose: To summarise, analyse and assess literary texts.

Text Structure	Auntie Peg's Holiday
Context (background information and synopsis)	Auntie Peg's Holiday was written by Robert Coleby and illustrated by Sarah Wilkins. The book is about Auntie Peg needing a holiday. She'd never had one before because farms and holidays don't go together. So, since she couldn't go to Fiji, Fiji would have to come to her.
Text Description (characters, themes and effectiveness of text)	The book was funny because Auntie Peg always did things the hard way. Even though farms and holidays don't go, Auntie Peg was able to make her own holiday. I liked the way the illustrations were done because they put a lot of detail. For example, when Auntie Peg was doing her ironing 'the hard way' and the writing said 'leaves and bits of earth were in the clothes', Sarah Wilkins actually put them there.
Judgement	I'd recommend this book to all the family, especially farm families who need a holiday.

As you can see, Text 2.2 has a beginning stage which identifies the general class of thing which will be explained (volcanos) and then another stage which explains how and why volcanos come to be. Text 2.3, however, has a beginning stage which gives background information about the text and its producer, another stage which describes the main characters and themes and a final stage which evaluates the work overall. Notice that the name of each different stage describes how that stage functions to achieve the purpose of the text. Now let's look at the purpose and structure of some other text types.

Exercise 2.2

Read the two examples of text types which are provided below. Each text has been divided according to its structure, however, the different stages have not been named. Identify the social purpose and the text type of each. Then try to name the stages of each text according to how they function to achieve the text's purpose. When you have finished, compare your answers to those provided in the Appendix.

Text 2.4

Social purpose: ....

....

Text type: ....

Text structure	**Why hats should be worn in the playground.**
....	Students should always wear hats in the school playground to protect their skin and eyes.
....	Firstly, hats protect the skin from sunburn. As we know, lunch and recess are during the sunniest parts of the day. Without hats, students' skin would get very burnt and that could cause skin cancer.
	Secondly, hats can help prevent eye damage from the sun. Even on cloudy days there can be a lot of glare from the sun. Hats help to prevent some of the glare so that we don't have to squint and hurt our eyes.
....	In conclusion, hats should be worn in the playground at all times.

Text 2.5

Social purpose: ....

....

Text type: ....

Text structure	
....	Most of the world's flowering trees are distinguished for their shape and form rather than for their flowers.

.... *Nearly all of the broad-leaved species are deciduous and are members of the group of plants known as dicotyledons. More than half of the 200,000 dicotyledon species are non-woody herbs.*

.... *Narrow-leaved trees, conifers, are mostly evergreens and can be identified by their shapes, needles and cones. The conifers are classified into eight families.*

2.3 Text types and school learning

In recent years a great deal of research has been carried out to investigate the text types which students need for learning at all levels of education.[1] In the appendix you will find annotated examples of a number of these. Knowing the structure and language features of text types such as these is very important because it enables students to successfully achieve the outcomes of the school curriculum. Table 2.2 shows how these text types can be related to some important outcomes across key learning areas.

Table 2.2

Common curriculum outcomes	Text type
Classify and describe phenomena	Factual Description Information Report
Explain how or why things come/came about Explain impacts and consequences	Explanation
Describe changes over time Retell events in the past	Factual Recount
Evaluate, analyse and assess issues Argue a case	Discussion Exposition
Entertain through telling a story	Narrative Literary Recount Literary Description
Summarise, analyse and respond to literary texts, artworks or performances	Personal Response Review
Devise or follow a set of instructions and record steps taken to achieve the goal	Procedure Procedural Recount

Important text types for learning are included in most primary syllabus documents. These are often organised according to whether they are literary or factual. Literary text types, such as narrative, literary recount and literary description explore personal experience in order to evoke an emotional response. However, others, like review and personal response interpret other texts or artworks.

[1] Three important research projects which have investigated written text types in Australian schools are: the Writing Project (Martin 1993); the Language as Social Power Project (Callaghan and Rothery 1988) and the Write it Right project (Coffin 1996; Humphrey 1996; Rothery 1994). These projects all drew on Systemic Functional Linguistics (Halliday 1985) and Genre Theory (Martin 1993) to analyse and describe the key text types of primary and secondary schooling. Martin (1999) provides a comprehensive account of the development of literacy pedagogies associated with this research.

Factual text types function to present information for purposes such as describing, explaining, instructing and arguing. It is important to note that all text types, factual and literary, represent the perspective of the producer of the text. This perspective often needs to be questioned and challenged by listeners, readers and, when texts are multimodal, by viewers too.

It is important to remember that different curriculum areas also require students to use different text types. Text 2.2 *Why volcanic eruptions occur*, is an example of an explanation which is a text type used to explain phenomena in areas such as Human Society and its Environment (HSIE), Science and Maths. Explanations would rarely be found in English or Creative Arts, however, because these subjects focus on creating and interpreting texts rather than on explaining phenomena. Text 2.3 *Auntie Peg's Holiday*, is an example of a text type (review) which does play an important role in these learning areas.

Working with text types to support learning

Text types, like outcomes, build on each other to develop learning. Different learning areas combine text types in different ways within a unit of work, a textbook chapter or a self directed project. These combined text types are called macro text types or *macro genres*. Macro text types can be formed by adding simple text types together to achieve a broader purpose or by inserting (or *embedding*) stages of one text type within another. Text 2.6 is an example of an information report which includes a stage from an explanation. More examples of macro text types are given in Chapter 7.

Text 2.6: Information Report

Text structure	Telephones
General statement	A telephone is a device that transforms voices into electrical signals so that people can communicate over long distances.
Description (parts)	Telephones have a number of parts. On the outside of the handset there is a mouthpiece, an earpiece and a keypad. Inside the mouthpiece is a microphone which contains a thin plastic disk called a diaphragm. The earpiece contains a loudspeaker.
Explanation sequence	People talk to each other on the telephone through the microphones in the handset. The sound of the caller's voice causes the diaphragm to vibrate. As it vibrates, it generates an electrical signal that passes down the telephone line to the receiving telephone. When the receiving telephone gets the signal, the diaphragm in the earpiece loudspeaker also vibrates and recreates the sound of the person's voice at the other end.
Description (kinds of ...)	There are many different kinds of phones. Most home and office phones have keypads and many are now portable. Mobile phones are not physically connected to a network and can be used from almost anywhere. Videophones, which contain a small TV camera give users a chance to see each other.

Table 2.3

Unit of Work	State and Federal Government
Sample Outcomes • HSIE Stage 3	• Explains the structures, roles and responsibilities and decision making processes of State and Federal governments and explains why Australians value fairness and socially just principles
• English Stage 3 (writing)	• Produces a wide range of well-structured and well-presented literary and factual texts for a wide variety of purposes and audiences using increasingly challenging topics, ideas, issues and written language features.

Possible areas for investigation and action	Key text types
Identifying the responsibilities of the three levels of Australian government	Information report
Explaining how laws are developed and changed	Explanation (How focus)
Explaining the influence of citizens on the decisions and actions of their governments	Explanation (Cause and effect focus)
Exploring perspectives on an issue associated with one level of government	Discussion
Presenting views on an issue and arguing a case	Exposition (eg. letter to relevant minister)

Adapted from 'State and Federal Government' Stage 3 Units for Human Society and Its Environment K-6 NSW Board of Studies

Table 2.4

Unit of Work (English)	Picture Book Bookrap (Online book discussion)
Sample Outcomes (English Stage 2)	Reads independently a wide range of texts on increasingly challenging topics and justifies own interpretation of ideas, information and events
	Drafts, revises, proofreads and publishes well-structured texts.

Possible sequence of teaching and learning activities	Key text types
Send introductory email to other participants in Bookrap	Description (Factual)
Reading a range of picture books shortlisted for Children's Book Council of Australia awards	Narrative
Read background information on authors	Recount (Biographical)
Give personal opinions on favourite book and justify opinions Respond to opinions of other rappers	Personal Response
Explain how the techniques used by the illustrator and writer work together to create meaning	Description (stage of Review)
Critically assess one of the shortlisted books	Review

Adapted from Bookweek-Picture Books rap 2001. Professional Support and Curriculum NSW Department of Education and Training

Units of work are often programmed around combinations of text types. The programmes outlined in Tables 2.3 and 2.4 illustrate how a unit of work in both HSIE and English use a combination of text types for addressing syllabus outcomes.

Becoming familiar with a wide range of social purposes and the text types used to achieve them allows children to access learning across all areas of the curriculum. However, there are a number of important considerations for working with text types successfully. These include:

■ **Being explicit about the purposes and text types of set tasks.** Students need to be able to see how the text types they are learning connect with learning outcomes in all curriculum areas. While terms such as 'story', 'report' and 'essay' are often used in generalised ways for a range of tasks required by students, these terms can be confusing if they are not explained in the context of purposes and text types familiar to students.

■ **Building a common language for talking about text types (a metalanguage).** This enables students to reflect on their own and others' speaking and writing and become more aware of how to interpret and create text types.

■ **Encouraging students to experiment with text production.** It is important to make clear to students that the text types included in syllabus documents are prototypes and do not represent all the possibilities of text production. These elemental text types are often combined and manipulated in creative ways (eg. some narrative text types begin with the complication stage in order to dramatically get the reader's attention). Once students are confident at recognising and producing elemental text types, they can be encouraged to work with them for different purposes within and beyond schooling.

■ **Exploring grammatical features of text types.** While knowledge of text types and structure is a very useful 'way in' to exploring how texts work, teachers and students need a more detailed knowledge of *grammar* to really exploit the possibilities for interpreting and producing texts.

2.4 **Text types and grammatical features**

In the previous sections, we looked at the purpose and structure of different text types and the role of these in school learning. However, as we indicated, text types also have other distinguishing features, particularly when we begin to look at grammar. Let's have a look at some of the grammatical features of Texts 2.2 and 2.3 to see how they too, relate to the purpose of the text.

Text 2.2

Why Volcanic eruptions occur.

Volcanic eruptions often occur at the boundaries of two ···· present tense
colliding plates. These plate boundaries are called
technical term ······· subduction zones.

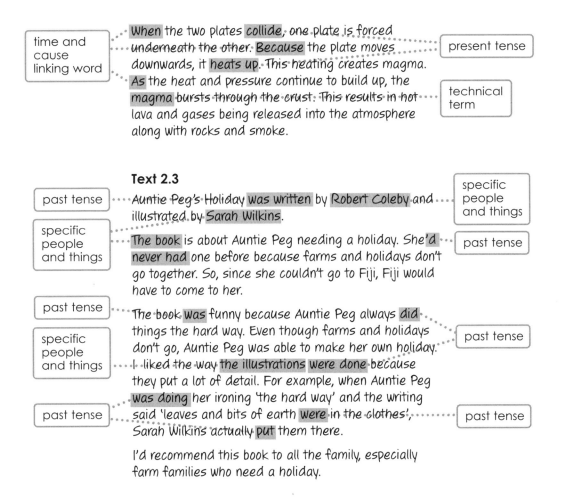

time and cause linking word — When the two plates collide, one plate is forced underneath the other. Because the plate moves downwards, it heats up. This heating creates magma. As the heat and pressure continue to build up, the magma bursts through the crust. This results in hot lava and gases being released into the atmosphere along with rocks and smoke. — **present tense** / **technical term**

Text 2.3

past tense — Auntie Peg's Holiday was written by Robert Coleby and illustrated by Sarah Wilkins. — **specific people and things**

specific people and things — The book is about Auntie Peg needing a holiday. She'd never had one before because farms and holidays don't go together. So, since she couldn't go to Fiji, Fiji would have to come to her. — **past tense**

past tense — The book was funny because Auntie Peg always did things the hard way. Even though farms and holidays don't go, Auntie Peg was able to make her own holiday. — **past tense**

specific people and things — I liked the way the illustrations were done because they put a lot of detail. For example, when Auntie Peg was doing her ironing 'the hard way' and the writing

past tense — said 'leaves and bits of earth were in the clothes', Sarah Wilkins actually put them there. — **past tense**

I'd recommend this book to all the family, especially farm families who need a holiday.

As we can see, Text 2.2 is written in the present tense because explanations are usually written about generalised events, occurring at all times. It includes generalised technical terms to build up scientific understandings. Linking words indicate that many of the events are related in terms of cause and effect.

However, in Text 2.3 the text is written mainly in the past tense because the writer was describing and commenting on events which were already completed. Unlike Text 2.2, Text 2.3 refers to specific named people. These are only some of the grammatical features which distinguish these two texts however, they are important ways of achieving their purpose.

The language in texts differs because of the choices we make from the resources of the language system. These resources are the grammatical structures and patterns which make different kinds of meaning. In the following chapters we begin to look at the basic building blocks of grammar and how they function to make meaning in both spoken and written texts.

Exercise 2.3

i. Look at your own outcome statements or syllabus documents for English and other learning areas. Find descriptions of text types which relate to your stage or area of teaching.

ii. Start collecting examples of text types which can be used as models in the classroom. These might include examples of text types which are structured effectively to achieve their purpose, texts which are not effective and texts which have combined or manipulated the elemental text types in an effective way.

iii. Use the following table to record your understanding of the key terms introduced in this chapter.

Term	Your understanding of the term
Text types or genres	
Culture	
Social purpose	
Text structure	
Stages	
Factual text types	
Literary text types	
Multimodal texts	
Metalanguage	
Prototype text types	
Macro text types	

iv. Look for further examples and descriptions of text types from any of the following references:

Building Understandings in Literacy and Teaching (BUILT) (2002) (2nd Edition) Love, K., Pigdon, K., Baker, G. & Hamston, J., CD ROM resource, The University of Melbourne, Melbourne University Publishing <http://www.mup.unimelb.edu.au/e-showcase>

Butt, D., Fahey, R., Feez, S., Spinks, S., Yallop, C. (2000) *Using Functional Grammar: An Explorer's Guide*, National Centre for English Language Teaching and Research, Macquarie University, Second Edition, Chapters 8-10.

Derewianka, B. (1991) *Exploring How Texts Work*, Sydney: PETA.

NSW Board of Studies (1998) *English K-6 Syllabus and Support Documents* <http://www.bosnsw-k6.nsw.edu.au>

Feez, S. & Joyce, H. (1998) *Writing Skills: Narrative & Non-Fiction Text Types*, Phoenix Education, Albert Park, Australia.

Priority Schools Funding Program (2002) *Reading texts in Stages 3 and 4: Science, History and Geography*, CD ROM Database of text types, NSW Department of Education and Training.

Unsworth, L. (2001) *Teaching Multiliteracies Across the Curriculum,* Open University Press, Buckingham, UK, Chapter 4.

3 Grammar and the organisation of meaning

Grammar is central to the organisation of language and meaning. Knowledge of grammar allows us to analyse and describe the ways in which words are selected, organised and sequenced within a text to make meaning. In this chapter we explore the different levels of the language system and introduce the 'building blocks' of the English language—the different grammatical structures that help 'package' meaning.

3.1 Building on traditional approaches to grammar

Many traditional and formal approaches to grammar have a tendency to focus on rules of syntax (how individual words are related in a sentence), word usage and written conventions such as punctuation, spelling etc. This kind of orientation has led many of us to see grammar as a prescriptive set of rules about how we should use language rather than as a resource for achieving different social purposes.

You may already be familiar with some of the traditional grammatical classifications of words such as noun, verb, adverb etc. These are often referred to as 'parts of speech' although they are in fact a part of both spoken and written language. A brief summary of these word classes is given in Table 3.1.

While it is useful to be able to identify a word in terms of its class, this tells us little about how these individual words combine to make meaning. It is the larger 'chunks' of language (like clauses, word groups and phrases) that form meaningful message structures. **These larger units are the grammatical structures used to package or organise the resources of the language system in a way that helps us achieve the various purposes for which we use language**.

Table 3.1

Word Class	Description	Examples
Noun	a word which names people, things, ideas, or qualities	boat, telephone, sausage, cyclone, discussion, disaster
Pronoun	a word used instead of a noun	it, that, he/she/they, those, them, this
Verb	a word used to say what someone or something does, what they are or what happens to them	eat, search, slice, drive, discuss, think, talk, is, has, like, laugh, sneeze, cause
Adverb	a word that tells something about a verb or adjective to indicate such things as when, how, where or in what circumstances	slowly, carefully, quickly, soon, now, overhead, beautifully, occasionally
Adjective	a word used to tell you more about a person or thing	green, dusty, enormous, old, smelly, tall, sharp, frightening
Article	'a', 'an' or 'the' placed before a noun to introduce a person or thing	There are only three articles: a, an, the
Preposition	a word that begins a phrase used to talk about place, time, manner etc.	on, in, for, from, by, at, onto, above, after, to, below
Conjunction	a word used to link two clauses, groups or words.	and, but, or, then, if, also, when, because

Building blocks: the clause

A **clause** is one of the most important grammatical structures—it is the basic unit of meaning. Each clause in a text contributes to the overall meaning and helps the text achieve its purpose. Clauses then, can be seen as the building blocks of a text. They join together to form sentences which in turn combine to form paragraphs and thus the stages in spoken and written texts. The way in which clauses help 'build' larger units of language is illustrated in Figure 3.1.

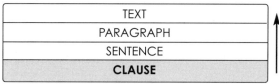

Figure 3.1

The following segment of text containing only one paragraph, has been 'pulled apart' to show the building blocks at each level. Note that the first two sentences consist of only one clause while sentences 3 and 4 consist of two clauses linked together by a conjunction.

T E X T	Sally is a mining engineer. She works at an iron ore mine in Western Australia. She takes rock samples from various sites and tests them in a laboratory. The job is challenging but Sally enjoys working in the great outdoors.

T	Sentence 1	clause	Sally is a mining engineer.
E	Sentence 2	clause	She works at an iron ore mine in Western Australia.
	Sentence 3	clause	She takes rock samples from various sites
X		clause	**and** tests them in a laboratory.
	Sentence 4	clause	The job is challenging
T		clause	**but** Sally enjoys working in the great outdoors.

Building blocks: groups and words

We can also look at the building blocks or **constituents** of a clause. Clauses are made up of one or more **groups**, which in turn consist of one or more **words**. When we analyse texts, we can then look at the choice, patterning and function of the groups in each clause, or alternatively, the words in various groups. Figure 3.2 shows how meanings get 'packaged' in a clause to form a message.

CLAUSE					
GROUP		GROUP		GROUP	
WORD	WORD	WORD	WORD	WORD	WORD

Figure 3.2

Let's now take two of the clauses from our earlier example and pull them apart. Doing this shows how the various groups in a clause consist of one or more building blocks from the level below, in this case individual words.

Clause	Sally is a mining engineer.				
Group	Sally	is	a mining engineer.		
Word	Sally	is	a	mining	engineer.

Clause	She takes rock samples from various sites.					
Group	She	takes	rock samples	from various sites.		
Word	She	takes	rock	samples	from	various	sites.

So what makes a group? How do we know which words form part of a group? The simplest answer is to say that a group is made up of words that 'stick together' because as a group, they serve a particular function in the clause. For example, some groups may function to name events while others may name where, when or how the events take place. As such, any group in a clause can be replaced with another group functioning in the same way.

Exercise 3.1

Take the clauses in Table 3.2 and look at how each group can be replaced with another that performs the same job or 'function'. Note that in some clauses a particular group might consist of only one word, while in other clauses that same group might be expressed by several words. Some groups can be left out altogether. See if you can make up clauses to fit in the last two rows of the following table.

Table 3.2

Naming 'who' or 'what'	Naming the 'action'	Naming 'who' or 'what'	Naming 'where' or 'when'	Naming 'how'
The frog	jumped		into the pond.	
The children from next door	walked	their BMX bikes	across the road	carefully.
Christopher	might be arriving		soon.	
Wild and ferocious storms	destroyed	several homes	yesterday.	

We can also say that a group is potentially 'expandable'—we can add more detail to a group and it will still function in the same way. For example:

Naming 'who' or 'what'	Naming the 'action'	Naming 'where'
The frog	jumped	into the pond.
That green spotted tree frog	will probably jump	into the murky waters of the pond.

Can you expand any of the groups from the clauses in Table 3.2?

Exercise 3.2

The ordering of groups in a clause is not 'fixed'. For example, a group naming 'where' may appear at the beginning or at the end of a clause. Complete the exercise below by labelling the groups in each clause that name 'who' or 'what', the 'action' and 'where', 'when' or 'how'. Some clauses may only use some of these groups.

Example:

Gold	was discovered	in Ballarat	in 1851.
what	the action	where	when

Carefully	place	spoonfuls of the mixture	onto a baking tray.

During his early career	Nikolai Poliakoff	experienced	many hardships.

Mum	found	a packet of cigarettes	in his bag.

These are all important understandings for building a picture of how the language system works. The notion of 'building blocks' enables us to look at the different levels of language, and shows how the units at each level of the language system are made up of one or more units from the level below. At the same time we have also indicated that the groups that form a clause have an important role in terms of meaning; how they function in a clause. This will be covered further in Chapter 4. Let us now move on to a closer look at the various types of groups that form the building blocks of the clause.

3.2 Types of groups

A clause can be described as a grammatical structure in which several components of meaning are brought together to form a message (Collerson, 1997:79). As we have just seen, one of the major ways we build up the meanings in a clause is by adding different types of groups or by adding elements to a group.

A clause is essentially 'about' something, thus the main element is a **verb group**. This forms the core of the message and tells us what is 'going on'. We can therefore recognise a clause by the presence or absence of the verb group. Most clauses also contain one or more other groups. These might be **noun groups**, **adverbials**, **conjunctions** or **text connectives**. These groups cluster around the verb group to form different types of clauses and make different kinds of meaning.

A group is like an expanded word—each group contains one 'core' element and, when there are other words in the group, they expand or modify this element to help it do its job. Descriptions and examples of the different groups and their constituents can be found in Table 3.3.

Table 3.3: Types of Groups

Type of Group	Typical structure	Example
Verb group (vg) Used with a noun group to say what someone or something does.	Main element is a verb. May contain helper verbs (to do with tense or opinion) before the main verb.	The rains **come** in January. She _will probably be_ **leaving** on Sunday. Emily _won't_ **eat** her vegetables. The ducks _are_ **swimming** in the pond.
Noun group (ng) Names 'who' or 'what'	Main element is a noun. Often contains describers before the main noun.	**John** smelt _the_ **smoke**. _The old_ **woman** lived in _a pretty little_ **cottage**. **Wombats** are _nocturnal_ **marsupials**.
	May include further expansion after the main noun.	We saw _a_ **shark** _with razor sharp teeth_. Some fish eat _the_ **leaves** _of green algae_.
	A pronoun can also do the same job as a noun group.	**He** smelt **it**. **They** are nocturnal marsupials.
Adverbials Extra detail about the events ie. when? where? how?	**Adverb**: main element is an adverb. (adv.)	The police should have come **earlier**. Pat the dog **carefully**.
	Adverbial phrase: a preposition combined with a noun group. (adv. p)	Hot gases were released **into the atmosphere**. **In the tree** sat three noisy birds.
Conjunctions (conj.) _or_	A conjunction linking clauses within a sentence.	The wind howled **and** the lightning flashed. She likes carrots **but** hates broccoli.
Text connectives (conn.)	A text connective linking sentences or paragraphs.	Thousands of tourists visit the region annually. **Consequently**, tourist traffic must be regulated.

Exercise 3.3

Texts 3.1 and 3.2 have been divided into clauses with each clause on a new line. The clauses have also been divided into groups. Label each group following the example.

Text 3.1

On Tuesday our class visited the aquarium. We saw lots of sea creatures. A shark with razor sharp teeth was chasing a school of small fish but they swam away very quickly. Then some kids fed the dolphins. At the end of the day we were allowed to buy an ice cream.

Social purpose: ....

....

Text type: ....

Example:

On Tuesday	our class	visited	the aquarium.
Adverbial phrase	Noun group	Verb group	Noun group

We	saw	lots of sea creatures.

A shark with razor sharp teeth	was chasing	a school of small fish

but	they	swam away	very quickly.

Then	some kids	fed	the dolphins.

At the end of the day	we	were allowed to buy	an ice cream.

Text 3.2

Emma was hiding behind the door. After a while she peeked into the room and saw a giant with huge bulging eyes. He was wearing an old tattered coat and had a black patch over his left eye. When the giant walked towards the door, Emma took a deep breath.

Social purpose: ....

....

Probable text type: ....

Emma	was hiding	behind the door.

After a while	she	peeked	into the room

and	saw	a giant with huge bulging eyes.

He	was wearing	an old tattered coat

and	had	a black patch	over his left eye.

When	the giant	walked	towards the door,

Emma	took	a deep breath.

Exercise 3.4

Now make up clauses to fit the following patterns. One group in each clause has already been provided.

i.
	have	
ng	vg	ng

ii.
On the weekend			
adv. p	ng	vg	ng

iii.
Put			
vg	ng	adv. p	adv.

Many grammars describe the basic structure of a clause as consisting of a **subject** and a verb group. The subject of a clause names the person or thing that the clause is about. It is followed by a verb group, which tells us what the subject is doing. Sometimes the verb group is followed by another group called the **object**. The object of the verb is the person or thing *affected by* the action. For example:

The princess	slayed	the dragon.
Subject	**Verb group**	**Object**

The fox	chased	the tiny rabbit.
Subject	**Verb group**	**Object**

Some verbs have two objects, a **direct** object and an **indirect** object. For example:

The prince	gave	the slipper	to Cinderella.
Subject	**Verb group**	**Direct object**	**Indirect object**

The boy	cooked	dinner	for his mother.
Subject	**Verb group**	**Direct object**	**Indirect object**

Christopher	read	Emily	a bedtime story.
Subject	**Verb group**	**Indirect object**	**Direct object**

The structure of a clause can be made more complex by adding adverbials. Clauses can be joined together by using conjunctions. Understanding clause structure from this perspective is often helpful in identifying the difficulties a student may be having with sentence structure.

3.3 Types of clauses and sentences

We said earlier that a sentence can be made up of one or more clauses. In this section we look briefly at the different types of clauses and how these combine to form different types of sentences.

Simple sentences

A **simple sentence** is one which contains a single (main) clause only. Clauses that can stand alone like this are called **independent clauses**. Here are some examples of simple sentences:

The bushfires destroyed thirty hectares of farmland.
Decorate the cake with strawberries.
The boy knew the answer.

Compound sentences

A **compound sentence** consists of two or more independent clauses. Each clause is capable of standing on its own and each provides equally important information. The clauses in a compound sentence are often linked or joined together by conjunctions. Here are some examples of compound sentences:

Emily played with her dolls **but** Christopher watched a video.
Do your homework **or** tidy your room.
The fire alarm rang, the shoppers fled **and** the police arrived.

Complex sentences

In a **complex sentence** the main independent clause combines with one or more **dependent clauses** (sometimes called subordinate clauses). These cannot stand alone and elaborate on the main clause in some way by indicating time, place, manner, reason, cause etc.

Cats clean themselves **by licking their fur**.
The shoppers fled **when the fire alarm rang**.
Fleeing from the fire, the shoppers ran **to find an exit**.

Exercise 3.5
Text 3.2 has been divided into clauses. Using the table provided, label the clauses as independent or dependent. Then label the sentences as either simple, compound or complex.

Text 3.3
When tobacco burns, it produces soot, tar, and nicotine. All of these are inhaled into the lungs. Nicotine increases the heart rate and blood pressure and gives smokers an enjoyable 'lift'. The other important substance in tobacco smoke is tar, which leaves dark marks on the fingers and teeth of smokers. Tar damages the lungs, causing smokers cough.

Clause	Clause type	Sentence type
When tobacco burns,		
it produces soot, tar, and nicotine.		
All of these are inhaled into the lungs.		
Nicotine increases the heart rate and blood pressure		
and gives smokers an enjoyable 'lift'.		

The other important substance in tobacco smoke is tar,		
which leaves dark marks on the fingers and teeth of smokers.		
Tar damages the lungs,		
causing smokers cough.		

It is important to be able to recognise the constituents of a clause in order to understand how they are structured to make meaning within texts. In the following chapters we will further explore the notion of language as a resource for making meaning. In Chapter 4, we look at the grammatical resources available for representing our experience of the world. In Chapter 5 we explore those resources which enable us to interact with others. In Chapter 6 we introduce the resources we draw on in order to create coherent and cohesive texts.

Exercise 3.6

Use the following table to record your understanding of the key terms introduced in this chapter.

Term	Your understanding of the term
Word class	
Sentence	
Clause	
Constituent	
Verb group	
Noun group	
Adverbial	

(continued)

Conjunction	
Text connective	
Independent clause	
Dependent clause	
Simple sentence	
Compound sentence	
Complex sentence	

4 Representing experience

One of the ways we can look at a clause is in relation to how we use language to represent our knowledge of the world and make sense of our experiences. This is the **experiential function** of language. Experiential meanings are concerned with how we name and describe:

- what is going on (events, activities, behaviours or states of being)
- who or what is involved (people, places, things, concepts, etc.)
- the circumstances surrounding these events (where, when, how, with what, etc.)

The experiential meanings in a text are heavily influenced by the context in which the text occurs. In education, it is the key learning areas of the curriculum that provide this context. As we saw in Chapter 2, different curriculum areas require students to use different text types. However, the curriculum content also has a significant impact on the grammatical resources used to represent the knowledge and experiences within these texts.

In this chapter we build on our knowledge of grammar and look at how the different types of groups (verb groups, noun groups and adverbials) are used to express experiential meanings. We then take a detailed look at the grammatical structure of these groups.

4.1 Experiential meanings

What is going on

As we saw in Chapter 3, every clause is 'about' something and it is the verb group that tells us what is going on. It names the events, activities, behaviours or states of being that are central to the clause. Text 4.1 is from a postcard. The verb groups have been highlighted and as you can see, they tell us not only about what the writer has done, but what she has seen and how she felt about some of her experiences.

Text 4.1

Dear Mum and Dad,

We arrived in Cairns on Sunday and are staying in a small hotel next to the marina. It has a great pool and lovely tropical gardens. Yesterday, we snorkelled near the outer reef. Bob took some photos of the fish with his underwater camera. Tropical fish are amazing. Some are rainbow coloured and others have fluorescent stripes. Then Bob noticed two reef sharks near the pontoon and called the instructor. She said that they were harmless, but I still felt scared. I loathe sharks!

Love Emily

Because our experiences are so varied, verb groups can express many different kinds of meaning. They may be about doing, saying or sensing or they may express meaning about what something 'is' or 'has'. We sometimes refer to these as different types of *processes*. When we write or speak, the kind of verbs we choose are influenced by both purpose and subject matter. Let's look at the different types of verbs in turn.

Action verbs

These types of verbs are about actions and events that involve people or things. They tell us what is happening, what has happened or what will happen in the future. Here are some examples of clauses with action verbs:

The toad **was croaking** loudly.
Share prices **fell** dramatically.
The witch **tossed** the slimy brown toads into the cauldron.
Tighten your bike chain.
We **will fly** to Fiji on Wednesday.

Action verbs are important in many text types, particularly those that are 'event' based. For example, in narratives, action verbs play an important part in constructing the sequence of events or incidents that are unusual and problematic in some respect. In recounts, action verbs are important in the retelling of experience.

Saying verbs

Verbs can also express meanings about what we (or others) 'say'. This can include direct and indirect speech and various other kinds of 'verbal' expression. Here are some examples of clauses with saying verbs:

David **announced** his engagement.
The robbery **was reported** to police.
The poor old wombat **pleaded** with the dingo.
"Can you help me find my mother?" **asked** the little duckling.
The manual **doesn't tell** me anything.

Saying verbs are very common in narratives. Dialogue helps us get to know the characters in a story and gives us an insight into the relationships that develop between characters. Saying verbs are also important in news stories, where the journalist 'reports' on newsworthy events in terms of what people say, claim, announce, state etc.

Sensing verbs

Sensing verbs express meanings about feeling, thinking, knowing. They may also include verbs which involve our five senses. Here are some examples of clauses with sensing verbs:

The frightened little turtle **felt** tired and lonely.
Everyone **loved** the ice cream cake.
"I'm safe here," **thought** the boy.
Jack **remembered** his dream.
Suddenly, the children **heard** a strange noise.

Sensing verbs are often used in recounts and narratives where the writer or characters reflect upon and evaluate what has happened by expressing their thoughts and feelings. Similarly, they are sometimes used in expositions, discussions and response text types where the writer wants to state beliefs or ideas.

Relating verbs

Unlike the previous examples where people or things were involved in doing, saying or sensing, relating verbs link or relate two pieces of information or two 'entities' in terms of what something 'is' or 'has'. In this way, relating verbs help describe, classify, define and identify things and usually involve the verbs 'to be' and 'to have'. Here are some examples of clauses with relating verbs:

Dolphins **have** a powerful snout.
Helen Keller **was** a famous author and lecturer.
The outer reef **can be** dangerous.
Christopher **is** the tallest boy in his class.
Wombats **are** marsupials.

Sometimes other verbs express the relationship between two things. For example:

This process **is called** evaporation.
These substances **will become** porous over time.
Coelenterates **possess** a large central body cavity.
The wall of the eye **consists of** three layers.
The heat from the sun **causes** water to evaporate.

Relating verbs are particularly important in explanations and information reports. They help describe features and characteristics, introduce technical terms, provide definitions and relate cause and effect.

Another related use of the verb 'to be' is to indicate that something 'exists' by simply stating 'there is'. These verb groups are often used at the beginning of narratives, recounts and reports and are sometimes called **existing** verbs.

One upon a time, **there were** three bears.
There are many types of fish.
Last weekend **there was** a huge windstorm.
There is a spider on the wall.

Exercise 4.1

The verb groups in Text 4.1 have been highlighted for you. See if you can identify whether they are action verbs, sensing verbs, saying verbs or relating verbs. Label each verb group in the boxes provided.

Text 4.1

Dear Mum and Dad,

We arrived in Cairns on Sunday and are staying in a small hotel next to the marina. It has a great pool and lovely tropical gardens. Yesterday, we snorkelled near the outer reef. Bob took some photos of the fish with his underwater camera. Tropical fish are amazing. Some are rainbow coloured and others have fluorescent stripes. Then Bob noticed two reef sharks near the pontoon and called the instructor. She said that they were harmless, but I still felt scared. I loathe sharks!

Love Emily

Who or what is involved

Types of noun groups

Doing, sensing and saying don't happen in isolation. Actions and behaviours are carried out by people or things and often affect or involve other things. Generally, it is the noun group that names the people, places or things involved in the clause. These noun groups are sometimes referred to as the *participants* in a clause.

The three examples that follow are extracts from different text types and thus the noun groups in each (highlighted) are quite different.

Example 1

Bob took some photos with his underwater camera. Some fish were rainbow coloured and others had dark stripes. Then Bob noticed two reef sharks near the pontoon and called the instructor.

Example 2

Sharks are cold–blooded sea creatures. They have muscular streamlined bodies and breathe using gills. Sharks' skeletons are made of cartilage. Their rough skins are covered with denticles which look like small teeth.

Example 3

The unlawful killing of sharks is an important marine conservation issue. A decline in shark numbers may lead to the extinction of some species.

In Example 1 the noun groups name particular people, places and things and use everyday language. In Example 2 the noun groups refer to sharks in a general way and include some technical terms. In Example 3, the noun groups name and describe abstract phenomena.

Table 4.1 outlines some of the ways in which we can categorise the things that are part of our experience. These descriptions help us to look at the kinds of noun groups that are important in the various text types.

Table 4.1: Types of noun groups

Category	Examples
Living	wombats, plants, Jack, the fox
Non–living	cars, air, the moon, a book
Human	my mother, Jill, Mr. Smith, we, he/she, I
Non–human	a cat, many trees, air pressure, juicy oranges
Particular	the bus, that pencil, the witch
General	buses, pencils, witches
Everyday	tomato sauce, meat-eater, leg, areas
Technical	condiment, carnivore, appendage, subduction zones
Concrete	sea-creatures, textbook, oven, boat
Abstract	issue, concern, intensity, accumulation, arrangement
Objective	flood, fire,
Subjective	disaster, inferno

Adapted from Derewianka (1998:22-25)

Exercise 4.2

Some of the noun groups from Text 4.2 have been listed in the table below. Using Table 4.1 as a guide, choose the categories that *best* describe these noun groups.

Text 4.2

Mosquitos are insects. They have three body parts and a sucking tube (called a proboscis). Mosquitos lay eggs on the top of water. These hatch into larvae. When a mosquito bites you it gets very itchy. I've got two itchy mosquito bites on my ankle.

Noun group	Types
mosquitos	
insects	
a sucking tube	
a proboscis	
larvae	
you	
two itchy mosquito bites	
my ankle	

Notice how the noun groups in a text also reflect the way in which the subject matter is being approached. In Text 4.2 for example, the writer begins with noun groups that result in a generalised, technical and objective approach to the topic. However, this changes and the text becomes more personalised, everyday and specific. It is worth noting that this is not always appropriate. Generally, noun groups should be consistent and reflect the overall purpose of the text.

Participant roles

As well as looking at the 'kinds' of noun groups that represent our experience, we can also look at how they 'participate' in the clause (which is why we sometimes refer to them as participants). For example, the noun groups that are potentially involved with an action verb have a different role to those that are involved with a saying or relating verb. Table 4.2 includes some examples of how we could describe these 'participant roles'.

Table 4.2: Participant roles

Clauses with saying verbs		
The dingo *doer*	caught *action verb*	the poor old wombat. *done to*
Government troopers *doer*	imprisoned *action verb*	hundreds of Aborigines. *done to*
The shed *done to*	was flattened *action verb*	by strong winds. *doer*
Clauses with sensing verbs		
David *sayer*	will be announcing *saying verb*	his engagement. *what is said*
The treasurer *sayer*	promised *saying verb*	an end to inflation. *what is said*
The instructions *what is said*	were clearly explained *saying verb*	to the children. *receiver*
Clauses with relating verbs		
The frightened little turtle *senser*	felt *sensing verb*	tired and lonely. *what is sensed*
The children *senser*	heard *sensing verb*	a strange noise. *what is sensed*
The thunder and lightning *what is sensed*	scared *sensing verb*	the dog. *senser*
Clauses with relating verbs		
Dolphins *entity*	have *relating verb*	a powerful snout. *description*
Helen Keller *entity*	was *relating verb*	a famous author and lecturer. *description*
This process *entity*	is called *relating verb*	evaporation. *description*

Being able to identify different process types and the different roles participants are able to take in these processes is very important for learning. Firstly, it helps us better understand what's going on in the text (eg. who's doing what to whom). These understandings can also help us to take a more critical reading of the text. For example, there are a number of ways an author of a story book may position us to see women. Some narratives may portray a female character as the main 'actor' in clauses with action verbs (ie. the character that does all the work!) Alternatively, giving the 'actor' role to male participants and the 'goal' role to female participants may position us to see the women as more passive than men. Similarly, giving men the 'sayer' role more often lets the male be 'heard' and portrays the woman as silent.

Table 4.3: Types of adverbials

Meaning	Example
Place • Where?	Crabs are often found **in rockpools**. Spoon the mixture **into the muffin tray**. I found my shoe **under the table**.
Time • When?	Jim fed the cat **after breakfast**. **Last weekend**, we built a tree house. We moved to the city **in 1987**.
Extent • How far? • How long? • How often?	She jogged **for eight kilometres**. We had been driving **for three hours**. I practise the piano **every day**.
Manner • How? • By what means?	We travelled to Sydney **by train**. Close the door **quietly**. She marched **like a soldier**. Cut the cake **with a knife**.
Cause • Why?	Those fish will die **as a result of lead poisoning**. The concert was cancelled **because of the storm**. The park is closed **due to extreme fire danger**.
Accompaniment • With whom?	Platypus swam in the creek **with his friends**. Play this game **with three other people**.
Contingency • Under what conditions? • Despite what?	Use the exit **in the event of an emergency**. We had fun, **despite the strong winds**.
Role • What as?	He came **as a clown**.
Angle • According to whom?	**According to experts**, the water level has fallen.
Matter • What about?	I'm worried **about the cyclone**. He questioned the boy **about the robbery**.

What are the circumstances

When we talk about different events, behaviours or states of being there is often a need to specify where, when, how, with whom etc. These are referred to as *circumstances* and are typically expressed by adverbials. Adverbials allow us to add meaning to a clause by locating events in time and space or describing the surrounding conditions or circumstances. Table 4.3 shows the different meanings that adverbials can add to a clause.[1]

---

[1] See Derewianka (1998:76) for further examples of adverbials.

Exercise 4.3

The adverbials in Text 4.1 have been highlighted. Use the examples in Table 4.3 to help you label the adverbials.

Text 4.1

Dear Mum and Dad,

We arrived in Cairns on Sunday and are staying in a small hotel next to the marina. It has a great pool and lovely tropical gardens. Yesterday, we snorkelled near the outer reef. Bob took some photos of the fish with his underwater camera. Tropical fish are amazing. Some are rainbow coloured and others have fluorescent stripes. Moments later Bob noticed two reef sharks near the pontoon and called the instructor. She said that they were harmless, but I still felt scared. I loathe sharks!

Love Emily

i. What role do adverbials play in Text 4.1?

....

....

....

....

Adverbials are important resources for building meaning in many text types. In Text 4.1, a recount, adverbials of time and place help locate events. In procedural texts, adverbials of manner, place and extent help with the precise nature of instructions. In more complex information reports, they can add extra detail to descriptions in terms of place and manner. In explanations, adverbials to do with time, cause and manner help link the events in a sequence and explain cause/effect relationships.

4.2 **Looking at grammatical structure**

Now that we have a greater understanding of how verb groups, noun groups and adverbials express different meanings in a clause, let's look at the grammatical structure of these groups in detail. This will help you to identify these elements in the texts children read and produce.

Grammatical structure of the verb group

As we have seen, verb groups express many different processes. Verb groups may consist of a **main verb** only, or they may consist of the main verb plus helper verbs (called **auxiliary verbs**). The main verb tells us what kind of meaning is being expressed (action, sensing, saying etc.). The auxiliary verbs tell us about tense or the degree of obligation or certainty involved. A negative can be formed by putting 'not' after the helper verbs. Here are some examples:

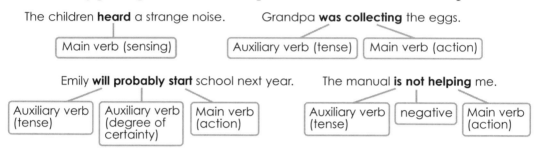

Other verb forms can also contribute to the complexity in the verb group. Sometimes the verb group consists of two verbs other than auxiliaries. These form a **complex verb** which expresses the one meaning. Here are some examples of complex verbs:

The python **began swallowing** the monkey.

Complex Action verb

She **tried to catch** her brother.
It **started raining** this morning.
The children **practised singing** all week.

Note that these complex verbs can combine with auxiliaries to form quite lengthy verb groups:

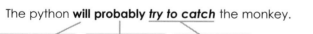

The coach **might have been *waiting to start*** the race.
Sarah **should be *allowed to leave***.
They **had not *finished washing*** the car.

The other kind of verb that can form part of the verb group is a **phrasal verb**. These consist of a main verb plus a preposition, but together express the one meaning. Again, phrasal verbs can combine with auxiliaries. Here are some examples of phrasal verbs:

The slightest noise **could <u>scare away</u>** the fish.

Lizards **<u>live on</u>** small insects.
We **should not <u>put off</u>** the decision any longer.
The council **might be going <u>to knock down</u>** the building.

> It is difficult to identify the main verb group in some dependent clauses, where the verb is in the form verb+ing (licking, fleeing) or to+verb (to find). For example:
>
> Cats clean themselves   by *licking* their fur.
> *Fleeing* from the fire,   I tripped over a rock.
> The shoppers ran   *to find* an exit.

Exercise 4.4

Highlight the verb groups in Text 4.3. Circle the main verb in each and label it according to whether it is action, saying, sensing or relating.

> **Text 4.3**
>
> We had been driving across the savannah for days. Having modified our four wheel drive, the film crew could sit on top. Suddenly our guide shouted. In the distance, a herd of buffalo began to cross the river. Something had probably frightened them. As we watched, many of the younger buffalo were being swept away by the current.

Grammatical structure of the noun group

Noun groups name the people, places, things or ideas which are involved in the clause. They are sometimes called *nominal groups*. As we have seen, a noun group may consist of the **main noun (or pronoun)** only, or it may be expanded by adding information **before** the main noun and **after** it.

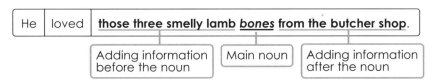

We can use probe questions to examine the kind of information provided by each element in the noun group. This is illustrated in Table 4.4.

Table 4.4: Structure of the noun group

Probe	Example
What?	**bones** (main noun)
Which one/s or whose?	*those* **bones**
How many?	those *three* **bones**
What like?	those three *smelly* **bones**
What kind?	those three smelly *lamb* **bones**
More details after the main noun?	those smelly lamb **bones** *from the butcher shop*

As you can see, the elements that cluster around the main noun provide many different types of information. We will refer to those words which provide information about a noun as **adjectivals**. Table 4.5 provides a summary of those adjectivals that come before a noun.

Table 4.5: Types of Adjectivals

Probe question	Function	Type of Adjectival	Examples
Which one/s or whose?	To point to or specify the noun being referred to	Determiner	this, his, my, John's, the, some, a/an, that, these
How many?	To give numerical information about quantity or order	Quantity adjective	six, four, first, several, many, all, a lot of
What like?	To describe or compare attributes and qualities of the noun	Opinion adjective	worst, smelly, fantastic, difficult
		Factual adjective	green, tallest, old, dusty, healthy
What kind or type?	To identify the noun as belonging to a particular group or class of things	Classifier	<u>fruit</u> trees <u>native</u> animals <u>science</u> book

It is important to remember that adjectivals are a *resource* for making meaning; we make choices to suit our particular purpose. It is also important to remember that there is a set order to the adjectivals in a noun group, and that we sometimes use several of the one kind. Table 4.6 shows the structure of a number of example noun groups.

Table 4.6: Example noun groups

Determiner	Quantity adjective	Opinion adjective/s	Factual adjective/s	Classifier/s	Main noun
these				marine-dwelling, carnivorous	molluscs
Jenny's		smelly	old	soccer	boots
	a few	important		political	decisions
the	last			date	scone
	three	ugly			ducklings
a			small, green		apple

1. We can sometimes *intensify* or *emphasise* opinion and factual adjectives in the noun group:
a) Intensifiers: a **very** old building; an **extremely** long snake; a **really** disgusting smell
b) Emphasising adjectives: a **total** disaster; a **complete** mess; an **absolute** terror

2. A combination of noun groups may function to name the one participant in a clause. For example:
The peregrine falcon and southern sea eagle are birds of prey.
The hunters shot **four lions, two cheetahs and several impala.**

3. Similarly, two adjectives joined by a conjunction may express the quantity, description or classification of the main noun. For example:
three or four white-tipped reef sharks   (quantity)
an **interesting but expensive** solution   (description)
the small **orange and apple** trees   (classification)

The information that comes after the noun can be expressed by an **adjectival phrase** or an **adjectival clause**. These are sometimes called *qualifiers* because they further qualify or define the meaning of the main noun. Adjectival phrases consist of a preposition plus a noun group. Adjectival clauses contain a verb (and are sometimes called *embedded clauses*). Both form part of the noun group.

Noun groups including an adjectival phrase after the noun:

a good exercise **for the spine**
the spectacular sight **of the fire**
temperatures **on the polar plateau**
a shark **with razor sharp teeth**

Noun groups including an adjectival clause after the noun:

the long tentacles **surrounding their mouth**
plants **that contain chlorophyll**
an old woman **who lived in a shoe**
the town **where I was born**

The resources of the noun group are important in both factual and literary text types. In factual texts, the noun groups package much of the 'content' that is important in the various key learning areas. In literary texts, noun groups are the vehicle for creative expression and play a vital role in characterisation and imagery.

Exercise 4.5

Following the example, describe the structure of the noun groups in **bold** in Text 4.4 and Text 4.5. What difference do you notice? Why?

Text 4.4

After watching **the spectacular sight of the fire** we were told **some news that was frightening**. The fire was heading towards our homes. It was **a horrifying thought**. **The local fire brigade** battled **the fierce heat**. We began to wonder whether our homes would survive **this dreadful natural disaster**.

Example:

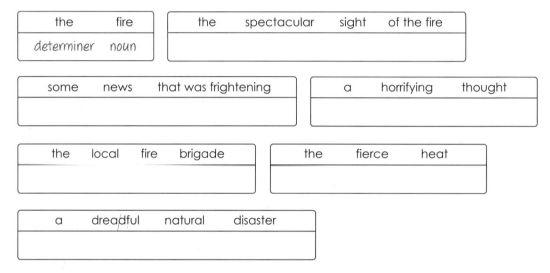

the	fire
determiner	noun

the	spectacular	sight	of the fire

some	news	that was frightening

a	horrifying	thought

the	local	fire	brigade

the	fierce	heat

a	dreadful	natural	disaster

Text 4.5

Fires are usually started by **an external heat source**. **One factor which affects fire behaviour** is **the moisture content of the fuel**. **Very fine fuels like grasses** lose moisture quickly. **The windspeed at the fire front** is also **an important consideration**.

an	external	heat	source

One	factor	which affects fire behaviour

the	moisture	content	of the fuel

very	fine	fuels	like grasses

the	windspeed	at the fire front

an	important	consideration

You may have noticed that nearly all the main nouns in Text 4.5 name abstract concepts and processes: *source, factor, content, windspeed* and *consideration*. An important resource for creating abstract and technical nouns like these is **nominalisation**. Nominalisation works by turning words that are not normally nouns into nouns. For example:

employ (verb) ➔ employment (noun)
tense (adjective) ➔ tension (noun)
verify (verb) ➔ verification (noun)
expensive (adjective) ➔ expense (noun)

These abstract nouns can then be described by adjectivals, thus creating nominal groups that name abstract concepts and phenomena like those in Text 4.5. Nominalisation is an important resource for condensing information in texts and is one of the major differences between spoken and written language (see Chapter 6 for more about nominalisation).

It is not always a noun group that names the 'who' or 'what' in a clause. Sometimes a whole clause is used to name the participant. (This is another kind of *embedded* clause).

I like **walking in the rainforest**.
Scrubbing with water and bleach is an effective solution.

In clauses with relating verbs, the description is often expressed by an adjective, not a noun group:

The film was **boring**.
Wombat's claws are **sharp**.

Grammatical structure of adverbials

The circumstances in a clause are typically expressed by adverbials. There are two types of adverbials: **adverbs** and **adverbial phrases**. Adverbs usually consist of a single word and sometimes end in -ly (eg. *slowly, briefly*). Adverbial phrases consist of a preposition plus a noun group (eg. *with care, in the park*). Table 4.7 gives examples of both kinds of adverbials.[2]

[2] For an extensive list of adverbials see Derewianka (1998:76)

Table 4.7

Adverbials		
Adverbs	**Adverbial phrase**	
downstairs, nearby, here, there, yesterday, any longer, slowly, angrily, quickly, . . .	across the road during the holidays in 1835 behind the shed for an hour	every morning with a spoon like a soldier by train

Exercise 4.6

Highlight the adverbials in Text 4.6 and Text 4.7 and label them according to whether they are about time, place, manner etc. (see Table 4.3) Then answer the questions below. Remember, adverbials may appear in various parts of the clause (ie. not always at the end) and there may be several different kinds of adverbial in the one sentence.

Text 4.6

Place eggs, sugar and butter in a bowl and beat well. Add the flour and continue beating until ingredients are well combined. Carefully stir through the chopped fruit and toasted almonds. Place spoonfuls of the mixture onto a greased baking tray and heat in a hot oven for 15 minutes. When they are cool, sprinkle generously with sifted icing sugar.

i. What is the purpose of Text 4.6?

....

....

ii. What kind of adverbials are found in this text?

....

....

....

iii. How do the adverbials help the text achieve its purpose?

....

....

....

....

Text 4.7

Once upon a time, in the middle of a dark forest, there lived a small girl named Jane. She lived in an old tumble-down house with her father, her brother and three cats. One day, Jane's father went into the forest to cut some wood. By nightfall, her father had not returned. Jane and her brother decided to look for him. After two long hours, they heard a voice in the distance. It was their father! When they found him, his foot was trapped under a fallen log. They lifted the branch and helped their father up.

i. What is the purpose of Text 4.7?

....

....

ii. What kind of adverbials are found in this text?

....

....

....

iii. How do the adverbials help the text achieve its purpose?

....

....

....

....

....

Meanings to do with time, place, manner, cause and so on can also be expressed by the dependent clause in a complex sentence. In other words, the entire clause expresses the meaning, rather than an adverbial. For example:

Cane toads were introduced — *to control insect pests on sugar cane.*

Independent clause | dependent clause ('why')

Heat in a hot oven — *until they are golden brown.*

Independent clause | dependent clause ('for how long')

4.3 **Bringing it all together**

Table 4.8 gives an overview of how different grammatical resources are involved in the representation of experiential meaning. In representing our experience and knowledge of the world, the choices we make from the language system are not random, but patterned in various ways in particular text types.

Table 4.8: Summary of experiential resources

Meaning	Grammatical resources	Examples
Representing activities and states of being (processes)	Verb groups	The new kitten **chased** a mouse. I **like** swimming in the sea. Feral pigs **are** dangerous.
Representing people, places, things, ideas (participants)	Noun groups Whole clauses Adjectives	**The new kitten** chased **a mouse.** I like **swimming in the sea.** Feral pigs are **dangerous.**
Representing the surrounding conditions or circumstances	Adverbials: —adverbs —adverbial phrases Noun groups	Walk **slowly.** Walk **across the road.** **The next day**, he climbed the mountain.

Exercise 4.7

i. Text 4.8 is an example of an explanation. Some of the common grammatical features of explanations include:

- noun groups about generalised, non-human participants
- action verbs in the present tense to indicate what is going on
- relating verbs to link causes and effects
- noun groups with factual and classifying adjectivals
- use of technical terms
- use of nominalisation

Highlight and label examples of these grammatical features on Text 4.8 below.

Text 4.8
High Pressure systems

High pressure systems are masses of air which are falling. They are associated with stable weather conditions.

High pressure systems begin to form when air is not heated and stays cool. The cool air contracts and becomes heavy. When it becomes heavy it falls. As a result, pressure increases over part of the earth's surface. The increase in pressure causes stable weather conditions which produce sunny, fine days and mild nights.

ii. Text 4.9 is an example of a narrative. Some of the common grammatical features of narratives include:

- action verbs to name the events
- saying verbs to express the words spoken by the characters or narrator
- sensing verbs to express the thoughts and feelings of the characters or narrator
- noun groups about particular human and non-human participants
- opinion and factual adjectivals to describe people, places and things
- adverbials to describe the circumstances associated with the different verb types

Highlight and label examples of these grammatical features on Text 4.9 below.

Text 4.9

The Dark Gloomy Night

One dark night Jack and I were driving to the show. As we looked out the window, we saw lightning in the distance. We knew a storm was coming. The wind grew stronger and stronger then suddenly a huge gum tree fell behind us. Then a few seconds later another tree, fifty foot high, fell across the road in front of us. We were trapped! A spectacular bolt of lightning lit up the road ahead. Then we heard an ear–splitting explosion as another bolt hit the tree in front of us. We were terrified. "Look!" Jack yelled. "The tree trunk has been split in half, we can get through!" We started the car and drove through the gap between the shattered branches. As we drove along we realised that the storm had passed. Now there was an eerie silence. "What on earth is that?!" whispered Jack. We stared at the tall, mysterious figure standing in the middle of the road. I gulped. This was all we needed.

Christopher (Age 8)

Exercise 4.8

Text 4.10 was written by a Year 2 student as part of a unit of work on spiders. Answer the questions below to help you assess the outcomes achieved by this student.

Text 4.10

Trapdoor Spiders

Trapdoors are invertebrates. They are not insects because they have eight legs. All spiders belong to the arachnid family.

Trapdoor spiders have a light brown body and a grey cephalothorax. They live in a burrow that has a lid which is open at night and shut in the day. They eat big insects like moths and grasshoppers. They lie at the top of the burrow and grab them. They have poison and inject it when they bite.

Christopher (Age 7)

i. How has the student structured or *staged* the text?

....

....

....

....

ii. What types of verbs has the student used?

....

....

....

....

iii. Describe the types of noun groups used in the text.

....

....

....

iv. How has the student used adjectivals to name and describe things?

....

....

....

....

v. Has the student used adverbials to add detail to the descriptions? What types?

....

....

....

Exercise 4.9

Text 4.11 below was written by a student after an excursion to the zoo. The teacher asked the students to 'write about' their trip.

Text 4.11

The Zoo

Last week our class went to the zoo. We arrived at school very early to catch the bus. We saw lots of different animals and had a picnic lunch. I am going to tell you about the snakes in the reptile house. There were lots of awesome species of snakes. Snakes bodies are long and thin and covered with scales. One snake was eating a dead rat. It looked really gross. Then we saw a huge python. Did you know that some snakes use venom and others strangle their prey? Jack wants a pet snake for Christmas but luckily his mum won't let him.

i. What text type do you think the teacher expected the students to write? Did the teacher's instructions make this clear?

....

....

....

ii. How has the student 'written about' the trip to the zoo? Does the student's text have a clear purpose? Do you think it is a successful text? Why/why not?

....

....

....

....

iii. Underline the verb groups. How do the types of verbs and tense of some of the verb groups back up your earlier comments?

....

....

....

....

iii. Use a highlighter to mark the noun groups. What types of noun groups are they? Why do you think they are so varied?

....

....

....

....

iv. Are the noun groups simple or complex? What kinds of adjectivals does the student use? Why?

....

....

....

....

v. If the task was to write a recount, how could you help the student edit their text?

....

....

....

....

vi. If the task was to write an information report about an animal they saw at the zoo, how could you help the student edit their text?

....

....

....

....

Exercise 4.10

Use the following table to record your understanding of the key terms introduced in this chapter.

Term	Your understanding of the term
Experiential meanings	
Process	
Action verb	
Saying verb	
Sensing verb	
Relating verb	

Existing verb	
Auxiliary verb	
Complex verb	
Phrasal verb	
Participants	
Participant role	
Nominal group	
Adjectivals	
Adjectival phrase	
Adjectival clause	
Qualifier	
Nominalisation	
Circumstance	
Adverb	
Adverbial phrase	

5 Interacting with others

We can also look at a clause in relation to how we use language to interact with others—to negotiate relationships and to express opinions and attitudes. This is the **interpersonal** function of language. Interpersonal resources are concerned with how we:

- Structure clauses for different types of interactions
- Take particular positions (strong, weak or middle) in our interactions
- Evaluate phenomena for the purposes of entertaining or persuading.

In this chapter we will look at how both grammatical structures and the **lexis** (ie. vocabulary) express different interpersonal meanings. Understanding how texts work in this way is important for interacting successfully in different situations. Analysing how interpersonal resources are used to persuade or position readers and listeners to take particular stances is also important for developing critical literacy.

5.1 Structuring clauses for interaction

In any kind of interaction there are a number of ways in which we can exchange meanings with others. In order to do so, we use different clause structures. Table 5.1 shows some of the different ways of interacting and the structures that are typically used.

Table 5.1

Ways of interacting	Type of clause	Example
To give information	Statement (Declarative)	Sideways has great coffee.
To ask for information	Question (Interrogative)	Who makes the best coffee around here?
To ask someone to do something		Could you make me a cup of coffee?
To encourage someone to think about something		Have you ever wondered about the stars in the sky?
To make an offer		Would you like a cup of coffee?
To get something done directly	Command (Imperative)	Get me a coffee!
To express feelings in an emphatic way	Exclamation	What great coffee!

Note that there are a number of different types of questions, which require different kinds of responses. Some important types are:

- Rhetorical questions, such as 'Have you ever wondered about the stars in the sky?' Speakers and writers do not usually expect a reply to rhetorical questions.

- 'Yes/No' questions such as 'Is the coffee good at Sideways?' or 'Does Sideways have good coffee?' The usual reply for these questions is 'Yes' or 'No'. 'Yes/No' questions are often referred to as closed questions.

- 'Wh–' questions (eg. 'who?', 'where?', 'when?', 'why?', 'how?'). The reply to 'wh–' questions is more complex than a simple 'Yes' or 'No'. 'Wh–' questions are often referred to as open questions.

Questions can also function in other ways. For example:

- As polite commands such as 'Would you get me a cup of coffee?' In these cases, speakers (and sometimes writers) do not expect an answer but they do expect action to be taken.

- To answer a question in a tentative way. For example, if a teacher asked 'What's the capital of Australia?', a student may answer 'Is it Canberra?' In this case the teacher may answer 'Yes' to confirm that the information meets her expectations.

Exercise 5.1

Text 5.1 shows how different types of clauses can be combined in different ways according to the type of interaction the writer or speaker wants with the reader or listener. However, before we examine this in more detail, read the text and answer the questions about its context.

Text 5.1

What's in the sea?

Have you ever wondered what's in the sea?

Are there mermaids riding dolphins through the waves?

Or is there a lost kingdom lurking below?

No there's not!

The sea is certainly fascinating and mysterious – not because of mermaids and kingdoms but because of the wonderful sea creatures that live in it.

Like me!

I'm Dory and I'm a bottlenose dolphin.

I can certainly ride the waves – I often catch the waves in front of speeding ships and I can leap out of the water and do somersaults.

Want to come on a sea voyage with me?

Click me and let's go!

i. Where might you find a text like this?

....

ii. What do you think the text is trying to do?

....

....

Text 5.1 is an example of a spoken text which is used with visual images to introduce a CD ROM for children about sea creatures. It combines the purposes of giving information about things and entertaining or motivating children. Like many CD ROMs and web-based resources for children, this text is designed to be interactive. It therefore uses a range of clause types to elicit different kinds of responses.

Exercise 5.2

Examples of the different types of clauses used by the speaker in Text 5.1 are given below. Identify the type of clause and way of interacting for each example. Information about the first clause has been filled in for you.

Clause	Type of clause	Way of interacting
Have you ever wondered about the sea?	Question	To encourage someone to think about something.
No there's not!		
The sea is certainly fascinating and mysterious.		
Want to come on a sea voyage with me?		
Click me!		

As you can see Text 5.1 uses a wide range of clause types to engage the listener in the content and facilitate use of the CD ROM. Let's now look at the clauses in another kind of spoken interaction.

Exercise 5.3

Read Text 5.2 and answer the questions about how different clause structures are used for interaction.

Text 5.2

T: So, what can you see in the picture? Chris?

C: There are some kids at the skateboard park?

T: Good Chris, and what are they doing there? Emily?

P: (interrupting) That big kid standing up is smoking Miss.

T: Yes Penny, but could you put up your hand next time? And Jenny, leave Rosie alone … move over here.

T: Now what do you think about them smoking at the park? Yes Penny?

P: My brother smokes when he goes surfing with his friends and on the weekend mum found some cigarettes in his bag and he's grounded for 2 weeks.

T: Does your brother smoke at home?

P: No.

T: Why might Penny's brother only smoke when he's with friends?

i. Complete the table to show how these clauses from Text 5.2 are used for different ways of interacting.

Clauses from Text 5.2	Type of clause	Way of interacting
So, what can you see in the picture?		
There are some kids at the skateboard park?		
That big kid standing up is smoking Miss.		
Yes Penny, but could you put your hand up next time?		
And Jenny, leave Rosie alone.		
Does your brother smoke at home?		

ii. In what ways is this text typical of much classroom interaction?

....

....

iii. Comment on the clauses the teacher uses to 'manage' the classroom context.

....

....

iv. How would you describe the relationship between the teacher and students?

....

....

In Text 5.2, we see that the teachers and students also use different types of clauses for different ways of interacting. For example, questions and commands help the teacher to play her role both as initiator of discussion on a topic and as the regulator of behaviour (eg. *Could you put up your hand next time? And Jenny, leave Rosie alone*).

Different kinds of relationships between interactants can also be expressed through the way the speaker or writer addresses the listener or reader. Two ways of addressing the reader are:

a) Through **personal pronouns** such as 'I', 'you', 'we' 'us'. For example:

So, what can **you** see in the picture?
Now, **I**'m going to tell you a story:
In this book **we** will be looking at some forms of energy.
Let **us** look at another form of energy.

Personal pronouns help the speaker or writer to establish more personal relationships with their listeners and readers. In many text types, particularly written factual texts, readers are not addressed directly at all. This is because the focus is on providing information rather than on establishing a personal relationship. However, in some textbooks written for younger readers the writer uses personal pronouns to focus on building skills or giving instructions to the student.

b) Through using names or titles of some kind to address people directly—these are called **vocatives**. For example:

Jenny, leave Rosie alone.
That big kid standing up is smoking **Miss**.
Darling, make me a cup of tea, will you?
Dear **Sir**, I am writing to complain about ...

Some vocatives help to establish more personal relationships. For example, calling somebody 'Darling' is a sign of some degree of intimacy. However, vocatives can also express differences in age, status, authority and frequency of contact. For example, while a student at school is expected to use vocatives, such as 'Sir' or 'Miss' to show a relatively formal or 'unequal' relationship, teachers typically use the first names of their students and often address small children as 'Dear' or 'Sweetheart'.

Clauses for interacting in different text types

While it is common to use a wide range of clause structures for the purposes of entertaining, instructing or motivating, most factual text types are marked by their use of statements. This is because the overriding social purpose of factual texts is to give information through describing, retelling, explaining and so on.

Factual texts, particularly written ones, are generally described as impersonal and objective because the writers typically don't attempt to interact with the reader. Text 5.3 is an example of an explanation, which uses statements to explain the phenomenon of the weather.

Text 5.3

The weather

Weather begins with the sun. The sun creates winds, clouds, rain and storms as well as warmth. Countries which are located near the equator receive the strongest rays from the sun and so generally have sunny weather. Too much sun without rain, however, can lead to drought, which causes hardship for farmers and animals.

One factual text which does not use statements is a procedure. The purpose of procedures is to instruct or teach somebody how to do something and this is usually achieved through a sequence of commands. Clauses which express commands are known as **imperative clauses**. Text 5.4 is an example of a procedure.

Text 5.4

To make Luscy.

Beat 1 cup of yoghurt lightly.

Add 1 cup of cold water.

Blend in 2 tablespoons of sugar and mix together.

Serve with ice and a little rosewater.

In some expositions, writers and speakers also use questions and commands to interact with the reader or listener. This is because they want to persuade the reader to take action as well as to argue for a particular point of view. This can be very effective if the exposition is in the form of a letter directly addressing the person or body responsible for taking the action. However, in other cases, expositions which use too many questions or commands can appear overly personal and informal.

5.2 **Taking positions in interactions**

Another way that speakers and writers interact with their listeners and readers is by taking up particular positions or stances in statements, questions and commands. One way in which speakers and writers do this is by expressing different degrees of probability, usuality, obligation or inclination. This is known as **modality**. By using modality speakers and writers can indicate that they have a particular point of view about something and demonstrate an awareness of other perspectives. In this section we will look at some of the main grammatical resources available for using modality.

Modality: expressing degrees of definiteness

Speakers and writers take up different positions about a range of phenomena. They may express a position about how probable or usual something is when giving or asking for information. For example:

There are three **possible** reasons why deserts remain dry. (probability)
How **often** does Penny's brother smoke? (usuality)

or they may express different degrees of obligation or inclination when asking somebody to do something or making an offer. For example:

You **must not** trespass on school property. (obligation)
Would you like a cup of tea? (inclination)

Modality expresses strong, medium or weak positions and includes all of the choices between a definite 'yes' and a definite 'no'.

Exercise 5.4

Read Texts 5.5 and 5.6. Answer the questions which follow them.

Text 5.5

School violence

There are a number of possible reasons for school violence. Perhaps children who have problems at school or at home feel frustrated because they cannot solve their problems. They might not be able to talk to their teachers or parents and may sometimes feel that they have no friends. This frustration could possibly turn to anger and they may take it out on other people. Children who watch a lot of violent TV shows may think that violence is the best way to solve problems. Adults may need to help these children to express their feelings in a peaceful way.

i. What is the main type of modality expressed in Text 5.5? (eg. probability, usuality, obligation, inclination)

....

ii. Place a cross on the cline below to indicate how strong or weak you think the position of the writer is.

Weak position   Medium position   Strong position

◄───►

Text 5.6

Dear Minister,

I believe that Australia must accept more refugees into the country. We have learned that recently there are many people who have had to leave their country because of war or their beliefs. They could not wait to get visas or stay in camps for many years so they risked their lives to come to Australia. They would not do this if they did not have to. These people need homes. We must help them to settle in to the country, not send them away. Please change your policies about refugees before it is too late.

Yours faithfully

Ming

i. What is the main type of modality expressed in Text 5.6? (eg. probability, usuality, obligation, inclination)

....

ii. Put a cross on the cline below to indicate how strong or weak you think the position of the writer is.

| Weak position | Medium position | Strong position |

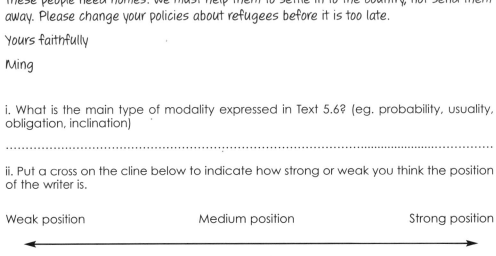

Texts 5.5 and 5.6 express different degrees of probability and obligation about the information they include. As with types of clauses, the degree of modality chosen by speakers or writers is influenced by how they view their relative status, power, commitment or expertise. For example, the writer of Text 5.6 has used a high degree of modality (must) in order to persuade the minister to act. This shows that he feels a high level of commitment to the information and that there is less room for disagreement. The writer of Text 5.5, on the other hand, may be indicating to their readers that they do not have a high level of expertise and are willing to negotiate with other viewpoints.

Grammatical structures for expressing Modality

Speakers and writers have a range of choices available to express Modality. They may take a strong, weak or medium position and express this position in more or less direct ways. In Chapter 4 we saw how grammatical structures such as verbs, adverbials, adjectivals and nouns were used to tell us what's going on in the text, ie. to express experiential meanings. Table 5.2 shows how these structures can also express different positions of the writer or speaker.

Table 5.2: Examples of Modality

	High Modality	Medium Modality	Low Modality
Modal Verbs (auxiliaries)	must, ought to, need, has to, had to	will, would, should, is to, was to, supposed to	can, may, could, might
Modal adverbials	certainly, definitely, always, never, absolutely, surely, in fact	probably, usually, generally, likely	possibly, perhaps, maybe, sometimes
Modal adjectivals	certain, definite absolute, necessary, obligatory	probable, usual	possible
Modal nouns	certainty, necessity, requirement, obligation	probability	possibility
Modal clauses and phrases (Interpersonal metaphors)	I believe (that)... It is obvious (that)... Everyone knows (that)... Researchers agree (that)...	I think (that)... In my opinion, It's likely (that)... It isn't likely (that)... If ..., then ...	I guess (that)...

Modal clauses and phrases (Interpersonal metaphors) are a more indirect way of expressing modality and are therefore often used to make texts seem more objective and difficult to argue against. Interpersonal metaphor will be discussed in more depth in Chapter 7.

Exercise 5.5

i. In Text 5.5, examples of modality have been highlighted. Use the table which follows this text to identify the type of modality, the degree, and the grammatical structure of these. An example has been completed for you.

Text 5.5

School violence

There are a number of possible reasons for school violence. Perhaps children who have problems at school or at home feel frustrated because they cannot solve their problems. They might not be able to talk to their teachers or parents and may sometimes feel that they have no friends. This frustration could possibly turn to anger and they may take it out on other people. Children who watch a lot of violent TV shows may think that violence is the best way to solve problems. Adults may need to help these children to express their feelings in a peaceful way.

Expression from Text 5.5	Type of modality	Degree of modality	Grammatical structure
possible	probability	low	Modal adjectival
Perhaps			
cannot			
Might not			
may			
sometimes			
could			
possibly			

ii. Text 5.6 also has a number of examples of modality, however only one of these has been highlighted. Circle or highlight other examples and then use the table which follows this text to record the type of modality, the degree, and the grammatical structure of these.

Text 5.6

Dear Minister,

I believe that Australia must accept more refugees into the country. We have learned that recently there are many people who have had to leave their country because of war or their beliefs. They could not wait to get visas or stay in camps for many years so they risked their lives to come to Australia. They would not do this if they did not have to. These people need homes. We need to help them to settle in to the country, not send them away. Please change your policies about refugees before it is too late.

Expression from Text 5.6	Type of modality	Degree of modality	Grammatical structure
I believe	probability	high	Modal clause

Modality and persuasive text types

Although modality is often used in literary text types, it is particularly important in factual text types which attempt to persuade the reader, ie. expositions and discussions. Unlike factual texts such as reports and explanations, these text types persuade the reader to agree with a particular position by building a picture about how the world might or should be rather than how it is. This involves using modality to temper or moderate both the judgements and recommendations so that they do not seem too extreme. Expositions and discussions can be made to seem more objective by using modal clauses such as 'experts agree (that) ...'; 'it is necessary that ...' and 'if ... then' clauses. Text 5.7 is annotated to show examples of modality in a persuasive text type.

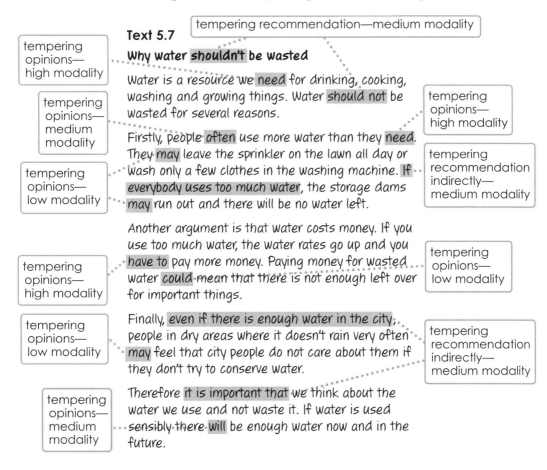

Text 5.7

tempering recommendation—medium modality

tempering opinions— high modality

Why water shouldn't be wasted

Water is a resource we need for drinking, cooking, washing and growing things. Water should not be wasted for several reasons.

tempering opinions— medium modality

tempering opinions— high modality

Firstly, people often use more water than they need. They may leave the sprinkler on the lawn all day or wash only a few clothes in the washing machine. If everybody uses too much water, the storage dams may run out and there will be no water left.

tempering opinions— low modality

tempering recommendation indirectly— medium modality

Another argument is that water costs money. If you use too much water, the water rates go up and you have to pay more money. Paying money for wasted water could mean that there is not enough left over for important things.

tempering opinions— high modality

tempering opinions— low modality

Finally, even if there is enough water in the city, people in dry areas where it doesn't rain very often may feel that city people do not care about them if they don't try to conserve water.

tempering opinions— low modality

tempering recommendation indirectly— medium modality

Therefore it is important that we think about the water we use and not waste it. If water is used sensibly there will be enough water now and in the future.

tempering opinions— medium modality

Taking a position by making a direct comment

In addition to using modality, writers and speakers can also take a position by using particular words called **comment adverbials**. Here are some examples of sentences with comment adverbials highlighted.

Unfortunately many of the baby seals died.
Apparently his mother forgot to pack his homework.
Curiously, he was well enough to go to the party but not well enough to sit for the test.
To be fair, it wasn't all her fault.

As these examples show, comment adverbials function to indicate to the reader or listener what the writer or speaker's attitude to the topic is. They often come at the beginning of the sentence and are used to persuade the reader or listener to see things in the same way as the writer or speaker.

5.3 **Evaluating phenomena**

In other sections of this book we have been primarily concerned with the function of different clause constituents. However, when looking at interpersonal meanings, it is also important to examine the way vocabulary is used across texts to make different kinds of evaluations. In this section we will look at vocabulary used to:

- Make positive and negative evaluations of people and phenomena

- Grade and intensify their evaluations

Writers and speakers use particular types of vocabulary in order to make positive and negative evaluations of a range of phenomena. This is called **evaluative vocabulary** or *Attitude*. Evaluative vocabulary can be divided into three categories, **Affect**, **Judgement** and **Appreciation**. Each of these categories plays an important role in learning in the primary curriculum. They are:

- Expressing feelings to build up empathy and suspense in stories *(Affect)*

- Making moral judgements of people's behaviour *(Judgement)*

- Assessing the quality of objects such as literary or artistic works, people's appearance or other natural or man-made phenomena *(Appreciation)*.

Although we will be looking at each of these categories separately, it is important to note that speakers and writers often choose vocabulary from two or three categories to create particular interpersonal meanings in text types. Examples of texts which use a range of evaluative expressions will be explored in section 5.5.

Expressing feelings through Affect

Affect is the name we give to the system of words and phrases which express feelings. Identifying the feelings of characters is very important for involving readers and listeners in stories such as narratives and literary recounts. Affect allows readers and listeners to empathise with characters so that they care what happens to them as they go through extraordinary events.

The writer of the following story has included a great many expressions of Affect to help the reader know and share the feelings of the characters.

Text 5.8

'Please fasten your seatbelts for take-off!'

This was it! Take-off! That dreaded word! The last of Amy's confidence evaporated and a wave of fear swept over her. Oh how she hated take-off! She fumbled nervously with the clasp of her seatbelt and then she grasped her father's hand as the great white plane moved slowly along the runway. Her father pressed her hand reassuringly but Amy was too frightened to look up at him. The plane picked up speed and the fear rose to pure terror in Amy's stomach. She stole an anxious glance around her—Gilly was grinning delightedly as she pointed out landmarks to an equally excited Andrew. How could they be so happy? Her mother, too, seemed relaxed and confident as she gazed calmly out over the water and her father... why, was that a nervous tick she detected on her father's cheek as he studiously studied the inflight magazine? Amy was momentarily distracted as she contemplated her anxious father staring unseeingly at the page, his hand growing ever tighter around Amy's on the arm of the seat. But then as the plane lurched into the air, her own fear returned with full force and the insides of her stomach churned like butter. Up! Up! Oh when would it stop? Her fingernails dug into her father's hand as the plane continued its ascent—higher, higher... and then

'Ladies and gentlemen, boys and girls! You may now unfasten your seatbelts and move around the cabin...'

It was over! The realisation hit her with a bolt—the anxiety vanished and she looked up excitedly. Her father looked at her a little sheepishly. Then they both laughed with relief.

'Whoopee!' Amy cried joyously, 'Currumbin Beach, here we come!'

Narratives are highly valued in the primary curriculum and students need to build up vocabulary for describing the feelings of characters vividly and effectively.

Exercise 5.6

Underline the words and expressions which describe the feelings of the characters in Text 5.8. Then use the following table to record the main feelings of each character at different stages of the story.

Character	Feeling/s		
	Beginning	Middle	End
Amy	afraid	terrified	relieved and happy
Father			
Gilly			
Andrew			
Mother			

As we can see the feelings of the main character and her father change as the events unfold in the narrative—thus helping to build suspense and to resolve the tension at the end. The writer also makes the negative feelings of these characters in the complication stage more vivid by contrasting them with the positive feelings of the other members of the family.

Types of Affect vocabulary

Affect can be further classified to describe particular positive or negative feelings which can be expressed by a range of grammatical structures. Table 5.3 provides an overview of the categories of Affect.

Table 5.3: A framework for analysing Affect

Emotional Categories		Examples
Happiness	(positive)	happy, laugh, love, hug,
Unhappiness	(negative)	sadly, misery, dislike, abuse
Security	(positive)	reassure, trusting, together
Insecurity	(negative)	frighten, tremble, fearful
Satisfaction	(positive)	engaged, attentive, impressed
Dissatisfaction	(negative)	to bore, empty, to enrage, embarrassed

Adapted from Martin (1997:22)

Exercise 5.7

Some examples of Affect expressions from Text 5.8 are listed in the box below. Identify the emotional category they belong to by writing them in the table which follows.

Expressions of Affect from Text 5.8

terror	confident	nervously	sheepishly	relaxed
laughed	grinning	excited	frightened	relief
anxious	dreaded	hated	joyously	calmly

Emotional Categories	Expressions from Text 5.8
Happiness	
Unhappiness	
Security	
Insecurity	
Satisfaction	
Dissatisfaction	

Grammatical structures of Affect

Affect can be expressed by a range of grammatical structures. The most common structures are shown in Table 5.4.

Table 5.4

Grammatical structures	Examples
Adjectivals	happy, sad, afraid, bored, empty, impressed
Verbs	frighten, enrage, bore, engage, laugh, hug, love
Adverbials	reassuringly, nervously, in despair, excitedly, joyously, with relief
Noun groups	laughter, fear, boredom, attentiveness, love, hate

Indirect expressions of Affect

The expressions shown in Table 5.4 are all direct or explicit expressions of feelings. However, you might have noticed that Text 5.8 also contained expressions which cannot be directly ascribed to one word or even a phrase. For example, the clause *she grasped her father's hand* expresses Amy's fear, through actions we associate with that feeling. Metaphors such as *butterflies leapt in her stomach* would also work to express feelings indirectly. It is important to remember that these meanings are very much influenced by cultural values and by the subject matter as well.

Exercise 5.8

Identify other indirect expressions of Affect in Text 5.8. Categorise these expressions according to their meaning.

Indirect Expression of Affect	Emotional Category
she grasped her father's hand	Insecurity

Affect and text types

As we noted earlier, Affect is very important for involving readers and listeners in stories such as narratives and literary recounts. It is also used in media stories to evoke an emotional response from readers. Affect is not generally valued in factual text types where writers attempt to build more objective constructions of reality.

Making judgements about people's behaviour

Another important category of evaluative vocabulary is called Judgement. Expressions of Judgement are used to assess (positively or negatively) what people do, say or believe according to values of particular institutions. Like the resources of Affect described above, Judgement can be expressed by a range of grammatical structures, both directly and indirectly. However, unlike Affect, expressions of Judgement are less obviously subjective because they are directed towards the person being judged rather than the person who is doing the judging. Expressions of Judgement are typically found in narratives, media articles and recounts (particularly historical recounts and biographies), expositions and discussions.

Exercise 5.9

Before we look at the categories of Judgement expressions in more detail, look at Texts 5.9 and 5.10 and answer the preliminary questions which follow.

Text 5.9

The Preamble to the Universal Declaration of the Rights of Man recognises that people should act kindly and tolerantly towards each other. People should treat each other fairly and justly without discrimination. The Preamble also recognises, however, that corrupt and cruel regimes have resulted in barbarous and evil acts and that it may be necessary to rebel against tyranny and oppression as a last resort.

i. What do you think the purpose of this text is?

....

....

ii. Are the evaluations mainly positive or negative?

....

Text 5.10

Pemulwuy

Pemulwuy was one of the most famous and effective Aboriginal leaders at the time of the first British settlement in Australia. He was a brave and intelligent leader who led the Eora people in a guerrilla war against the invaders.

From 1770 Pemulwuy organised many attacks against the British who had invaded and occupied sacred land. In 1797 he was shot and captured during a raid, however, he was so strong that he managed to escape from his chains. His ability to escape capture and survive made many British soldiers afraid because they believed that he was magic and could not die. However, in 1802 he was finally shot and killed by a British patrol.

Pemulwuy is a very important historical figure because he encouraged his people to defend their land and free themselves from white invaders.

i. Where might you find a text like this?

....

....

ii. What do you think the purpose of this text is?

....

....

iii. Pemulwuy's behaviour is evaluated positively by the author. How is the behaviour of the British people evaluated?

....

....

We can see that, while Texts 5.9 and 5.10 are both concerned with judging the behaviour of individuals or groups of people, there are differences in the values which are judged.

Types of Judgement expressions

Judgements can be of two different kinds. These are:

- **Social Sanction**—concerned with Judgement of morality or legality (ie. Text 5.9)
- **Social Esteem**—concerned with Judgement of personal things such as capacity, competence or psychological disposition (ie. Text 5.10).

Table 5.5 shows some of the choices available in these categories.

Table 5.5: A framework for analysing Judgement

SOCIAL ESTEEM (Personal/psychological)	POSITIVE (admire)	NEGATIVE (criticise)
Is s/he special?	lucky, fashionable, normal	unfortunate, odd, weird
Is s/he capable?	powerful, intelligent, skilled	weak, insane, stupid
Is s/he dependable?	brave, tireless	rash, cowardly

SOCIAL SANCTION (Moral and legal)	POSITIVE (praise)	NEGATIVE (condemn)
Is s/he honest?	truthful, genuine, frank	dishonest, manipulative
Is s/he good?	good, just, kind, noble	bad, corrupt, cruel, evil

Adapted from Martin (1997:23)

Indirect expressions of Judgement

As with Affect, expressions of Judgement can be made indirectly. For example, the clause, *he managed to escape from his chains* in Text 5.10 can be read as a positive judgement of Pemulwuy's capacity as well as to retell an event in his life.

Sometimes too, feelings can be used as indirect Judgements. For example, in a culture where courage is highly valued, a statement such as 'Many soldiers were afraid' would be read as a negative Judgement of tenacity (ie. weak). It is always important to remember that an understanding or 'reading' of a text might be influenced by such factors as our cultural background, class, age, gender and socio-economic status.

Exercise 5.10

Highlight the expressions of Judgement used in Texts 5.9 and 5.10. Use a different colour highlighter for expressions of Social Esteem and expressions of Social Sanction. Then fill in the table below with information about the patterns of Judgements used. An example from Text 5.9 has been completed.

Text 5.9

Person, group or institution who is judged	Main type/s of Judgement used	Positive or Negative	Examples
People	Social Sanction	positive	Kindly, tolerantly, fairly, justly, without discrimination
Regimes			

Text 5.10

Person, group or institution who is judged	Main type/s of Judgement used	Positive or Negative	Examples
Pemulwuy			
British			
British soldiers			

You may have noticed that in both texts the authors use particular types of Judgement for particular individuals, groups or institutions. For example, Pemulwuy is associated with positive judgements of both Social Esteem (judging his capacity) and of Social Sanction (judging his goodness). The British people on the other hand are mostly associated with negative self esteem (unable to capture him; afraid) and inhumanity. This contrast allows the authors to build up a vivid picture of the people and situation and also to encourage the reader to take a particular position.

Judgement and text types

The examples of Judgement we have seen so far in this section have come from factual texts such as expositions and biographical recounts. Judgement is important in these text types because it allows the writer to influence the reader's opinion about people and issues. Often Judgement is included in factual texts indirectly through the selection of some events which the writer thinks will show positive or negative evaluations of people's behaviour.

In literary text types such as narrative and recount, Judgement is used to build descriptions of characters (eg. heroic, evil, kind) so that the reader builds a strong relationship with them. In response text types such as review, writers use Judgement to make evaluations of the characters' attitudes and behaviour.

Assessing the quality of objects

A third type of evaluative vocabulary relates to evaluations primarily of objects, such as literary or artistic works, people's appearance or other natural or man-made phenomena. This category is called Appreciation. Like the other categories of evaluative vocabulary, Appreciation can be expressed by a range of grammatical forms, in both positive and negative terms and both directly and indirectly. Expressions of Appreciation are typically found in descriptions, narratives and response text types as well as in expositions and discussions.

Exercise 5.11

Before examining the resources of Appreciation in more detail, look at the two texts below and answer the preliminary questions which follow.

Text 5.11

Grandpa Bill's garden

My Grandpa Bill has a wonderful peaceful garden far away from the noisy, busy city. In his garden Grandpa Bill has planted lots of beautiful tropical plants which have bright colourful flowers in the summer and vivid green leaves all year round. Grandpa has a greenhouse in his garden so that he can grow rare and delicate plants like orchids. There are lots of special places in the garden. We love to run through the paths and hide from each other in the ferns.

i. What is the text type of Text 5.11?

....

ii. Underline the expressions the writer has used to describe the qualities of the garden.

iii. Comment on the kind of descriptions which are made.

....

....

Text 5.12

Fox

Fox is an interesting picture book written by Margaret Wild and illustrated by Ron Brooks. It is a story of a friendship between a magpie and a dog which is challenged by an evil Fox.

The illustrations in the book are very effective because they seem quick and rough but they are really sophisticated and full of texture. Oil and chalk and charcoal are used effectively to give a bushy feeling.

The writing seems messy like a draft but this matches with the outback pictures. The writing and pictures work together for the exact effect that the writer and illustrator wanted.

Fox is a beautiful and meaningful story, suitable for all ages.

i. What is the text type of Text 5.12?

....

ii. Underline the expressions the writer has used to assess the book.

iii. Comment on the kind of assessments which are made.

....

....

Descriptions like Text 5.11 and reviews like Text 5.12 describe objects in different ways. This is reflected in the different types of Appreciation expressions used.

Types of Appreciation expressions

We can identify different categories within Appreciation. These are assessments of:

- the emotional impact of the thing —**Reaction**
- how the thing is constructed—**Composition**
- the worth or significance of the thing—**Valuation**

Although some words and expressions are common to all topics and subjects (eg. *good*), others are quite specific to particular fields and purposes. The term *well-written* for example would only be used to assess a written text. Table 5.6 shows some examples of these categories which are typical of those used in description and/or response genres. The questions can be used to probe the kinds of evaluations being made.

Table 5.6: A framework for analysing Appreciation

Category	Positive	Negative
Reaction Did I like it?	good, lovely, enjoyable, funny, entertaining	dull, boring, smelly, weird
Composition Was it well constructed?	well-written, well-drawn, imaginative, effective, manicured, clean	simplistic, hard to follow, too detailed, untidy
Valuation Was it worthwhile?	challenging, profound, meaningful, worthwhile, unique	shallow, insignificant

Some expressions of Appreciation may be used in both a positive and a negative way. For example, it is possible to find the word *traditional* used both positively and negatively in reviews of stories or films. Readers who interpret an evaluative word differently are said to have different 'reading positions'.

Exercise 5.12

Some of the direct and indirect expressions of Appreciation in Texts 5.11 and 5.12 have been highlighted. Using Table 5.6 as a guide, label the type of Appreciation.

Text 5.11

Grandpa Bill's garden

My Grandpa Bill has a wonderful peaceful garden far away from the noisy, busy city. In his garden Grandpa Bill has planted lots of beautiful tropical plants which have bright colourful flowers in the summer and vivid green leaves all year round. Grandpa has a greenhouse in his garden so that he can grow rare and delicate plants like orchids. There are lots of special places in the garden. We love to run through the paths and hide from each other in the ferns.

Text 5.12

Fox

Fox is an interesting picture book written by Margaret Wild and illustrated by Ron Brooks. It is a story of a friendship between a magpie and a dog, which is challenged by an evil Fox.

The illustrations in the book are very effective because they seem quick and rough but they are really sophisticated and full of texture. Oil and chalk and charcoal are used effectively to give a bushy feeling. The writing seems like a draft but this matches with the outback pictures. The writing and pictures work together for the exact effect that the writer and illustrator wanted.

Fox is a beautiful and meaningful story, suitable for all ages. Although it seems to be so Australian, the story reminds us of traditional European fables.

i. Why do you think the two texts use different types of Appreciation expressions?

....

....

....

As you can see the writers of Texts 5.11 and 5.12 used different kinds of Appreciation expressions. Text 5.11 uses mainly reaction types of Appreciation to describe features of the garden to which she responds emotionally. Text 5.12, however, uses mainly composition and valuation to describe how the writing and illustrations of 'Fox' work to make it a successful book. Note that the writer of Text 5.11 has also used expressions of Affect (eg. We **love** to run through the paths) to give her emotional response to the garden.

Appreciation and text types

Appreciation (Reaction) is typical of the text types such as description and personal response which focus on the emotional reaction of the person describing or assessing the object. It is also used in narrative text types to set the scene and describe the physical features of people, places and things.

Appreciation is also used in reviews. In this text type, the categories of Composition and Valuation are more likely to be used as the focus shifts from the emotional response of the reviewer to evaluations of books, artworks and films as 'constructed text'. Students are also expected to make critical judgements about the text and its value. Encouraging students to use vocabulary from the Composition and Valuation categories can assist them to produce reviews which are valued at an upper primary and secondary level.

Grading and intensifying evaluations

One of the distinguishing features of evaluative vocabulary is that the meanings can be graded up or down. The most common way to grade meanings is from low to high intensity.

Exercise 5.13

Read through the following two versions of a story and answer the questions which follow.

Text 5.13

One night I woke up and wanted to go to the toilet. It was dark and I was scared. I walked down the hall and then trod in something slimey. I called out and Mum came running from her bedroom. She turned on the light and I saw that cat poo was on my foot! It was awful!

Text 5.14

One stormy night I woke up busting to go to the toilet. It was pitch dark and I was so scared my teeth were chattering. I slowly slowly crept down the endless hall and then Squelch! Something horribly slimey oozed through my toes. I let out an ear piercing scream and Mum came hurtling out of her bedroom looking like a ghost. She snapped the light switch to reveal runny cat poo all over my foot! It was so gross!

i. Do the two texts share the same purpose?

....

ii. Which text makes the events seem more dramatic or exciting?

....

iii. Circle any words or phrases which make this text more dramatic.

Grammatical structures for grading

The writer of Text 5.14 has used a number of resources to 'turn up' or intensify the meanings in order to make the events seem more dramatic. Some of these resources are shown in Table 5.7.

Table 5.7: A framework for analysing grading expressions

Direct grading	Examples from Text 5.14
Adverbial graders	I could **hardly** walk.
	It was **so** gross.
Adjectival graders	the **endless** hall, an **ear piercing** scream
Repetition	I **slowly slowly** crept down the hall.
Exclamations or Swearing	It was so **gross!**

In addition to the direct graders shown above, there are a number of **indirect** ways to 'turn the volume' of meanings. One important way is through grading the core meaning of a word or expression. This happens when you make a word more or less intense. Table 5.8 shows some of the graded words from Text 5.14 with some of the expressions which could have been used for more or less intense meanings.

Table 5.8: Examples of grading core meanings of words

Graded meaning (Turning up the volume)	Core meaning	Graded meaning (Turning down the volume)
sprint, dash, **hurtle**, charge	run	lope, flit, amble, jog, trot
ear splitting; raucous, thunderous, piercing, deafening	loud	stifled, muffled,
march, trudge, strut	walk	**creep**, saunter, stroll
endless, never-ending, interminable	long	
ooze, gush, spurt, pour	flow	dribble, trickle, drip

Note also that figurative language such as simile and metaphor can also function to turn up and down the volume of core meanings. For example, the simile 'looking like a ghost' is a way of intensifying the meaning of 'scared'.

5.4 Interpersonal resources and critical literacy

Understanding the resources of interpersonal language contributes greatly to the development of critical literacy. Through exploring how resources such as different clause types, modality, evaluative vocabulary, and grading work, students can gain great insights into how texts persuade and position readers and listeners in different ways. Although critical literacy will be addressed in more detail in Chapter 7, here we will illustrate how an understanding of the resources of Affect, indirect Judgement and Grading expressions can assist students to recognise how a powerful lobby group might disguise persuasion within a seemingly straightforward recount.

Text 5.15

Leonora Lee had always feared guns. She hated her husband's gun and worried about it being in the house. That was until the night of May 2nd when three armed robbers broke into her house, firing randomly. Despite her terror, Leonora reached for the hated gun and angrily fired five shots in the air. The robbers fled. Happily for everyone, no one was injured. "I still don't like guns and I'm sad that we have to live with a gun in the house", says Leonora, "but after that terrifying night, it's the only way I can stay here and feel safe."

This text could be described as a story or Narrative with the purpose of telling a story in order to entertain. However, Text 5.15 is adapted from a web site set up by a powerful lobby group which supports gun ownership. It is the first text on the web site and is followed by a number of expositions which argue that people should be allowed to own guns. In this context, it is possible to identify the primary purpose of Text 5.15 as persuading the reader to accept the need for gun ownership.

The interpersonal resources of language are also used in an interesting way in Text 5.15. Most obviously, the writer has used the resources of Affect to describe Leonora's negative emotions towards guns. While Affect certainly works to make the story gripping and entertaining, it is also used to help the writer build up the argument for gun ownership. By acknowledging the possible emotions of those opposed to gun-ownership, especially women, the writer seeks to establish an emotional connection and thereby to 'open the reader up' to changing their position on gun ownership.

An understanding of indirect expressions of Judgement can also help us to see how Leonora Lee's behaviour is constructed in the text. What seem like simple descriptions of events (eg. *Leonora reached for the hated gun and angrily fired five shots in the air*) can be read as courageous actions, especially when set beside Leonora's fear (eg. *Despite her terror*). In this way the reader is positioned to see using a gun as heroic (and in a culture which values heroism, justifiable).

We can note too, that the resources of Grading have been used to intensify the emotions in the text. The intensity of the emotion 'fear' is turned up as the story progresses to become *terror* and *terrifying* while the emotion *hated* is turned down to become *don't like* as Leonora (and the reader?) are led by the writer to accept the need for guns.

Readers who are aware of how these and other interpersonal resources are used by the writer have more choices in the position they choose to take up. They can accept the pathway set out by the writer or they can resist it and look for other ways to construct the events and arguments.

5.5 Bringing it all together

In summary, Table 5.9 shows some key ways in which interpersonal resources can be expressed. In order to complete the following exercises, you will need to draw on your knowledge of all the resources for interacting with others.

Exercise 5.14

Text 5.16 is an example of a literary recount. Some of the common interpersonal features of literary recounts include:

- Modality to express degrees of probability, usuality, obligation and inclination

- Comment adverbials to give the speaker or writer's opinion

- Affect vocabulary to express the feelings of the people involved

- Judgement vocabulary to evaluate people's behaviour

- Appreciation vocabulary to describe scenes and describe what things look like.

- Direct and indirect grading expressions to make evaluations more intense or less intense.

Highlight and label examples of these grammatical features on Text 5.16 below.

Text 5.16

When I was a small child my favourite activity was to watch my mother make meringues. Mum was a very creative cook and was especially famous for her meringues.

I used to watch very carefully while she skilfully beat the egg whites and folded in the sugar. She was very fussy and would get quite angry if I tried to sneak some of the mixture. I couldn't wait to see the perfectly formed shapes with their magical twirls emerge from the oven and to enjoy the sweet crunchy, melt in your mouth experience of eating them. My birthdays were never complete without a wonderful meringue pie towering with mile-high golden meringue.

(continued)

Unfortunately, even though I watched so attentively, I have never managed to make meringues as well as my mum. Maybe I'm just not patient enough.

Table 5.9: Summary of interpersonal resources

Meanings	Interpersonal resources	Examples
Interacting in different ways. For example: • giving information • asking for information • making an offer • demanding action	**Types of clauses** • Statements • Questions • Commands (Imperative) • Exclamations	 Spiders are invertebrates. Are spiders insects? Put that spider down! What a horrible spider!
To take up particular high, medium or low positions. For example: • probability • usuality • obligation • inclination	**Modality** • Modal verbs • Modal adverbials • Modal adjectivals • Modal nouns • Modal clauses and phrases **Comment Adverbials**	 We **shouldn't** kill spiders. Spiders **rarely** attack. It's an **absolute** fact. It is **my duty** to protect you. **I think** spiders are great. **Happily**, no one was hurt.
To evaluate phenomena positively or negatively. For example: • Expressing feelings • Making moral judgements of people's behaviour • Assessing the quality of artistic works, people's appearance or other natural or man-made phenomena	**Evaluative Vocabulary** **Affect** • Happiness/unhappiness • Security/insecurity • Satisfaction/dissatisfaction **Judgement** • Social Sanction • Social esteem **Appreciation** • Reaction • Composition • Valuation	 She **loved** the garden. She fought **courageously**. She had a **fear** of spiders. **The robbers fled.** Hagrid **cared** for the spiders. It was a **lovely** garden. It had a **manicured** lawn. **It inspired peace.**
To grade and intensify evaluations of phenomena	**Direct graders** • Adverbial graders • Adjectival graders • Repetition • Exclamations or swearing **Indirect graders** • Core meaning graded up • Core meaning graded down	 It was **incredibly** big. That's **fabulous**! **Yummy yummy**! **No! You're kidding!** Water **gushed** from the pipe. Water **trickled** from the pipe.

Exercise 5.15

Text 5.17 is an example of a discussion. Some of the common interpersonal features of discussions include:

- Statements to build an impersonal and objective relationship with the reader or listener
- Modality to express degrees of probability, usuality and obligation
- Judgement vocabulary to evaluate the behaviour of groups of people
- Appreciation vocabulary to assess significance and importance
- Direct and indirect grading expressions to make evaluations more intense or less intense.

Highlight and label examples of these grammatical features on Text 5.17 below.

Text 5.17

In recent years there has been a great deal of debate over whether rainforests should be logged. The logging industry thinks that logging is necessary for employment and the economy while conservationists believe that rainforests need to be protected as habitats for valuable plants and wildlife.

The main argument for why logging should continue is that the rainforest logging industry creates many jobs for people and also supports the economy of many small towns. If logging is stopped, many workers will lose their jobs. That will lead to significant social upheaval for the workers and could, in some cases, result in the death of 'mill' towns.

On the other hand, rainforests are extremely important to maintaining the diversity of Australian plant and wildlife species. Logging is already placing the delicate rainforest ecosystem at risk. In addition to destroying irreplaceable trees, logging operations kill many animals directly and also indirectly by destroying their habitats.

After considering the arguments of both the logging industry and conservations, it is clear that the issues at stake are not simple. Employment is very important to rural Australia, however, our environment is priceless. One solution could be to phase out logging gradually and develop eco-tourism to provide employment for local communities. This could be a way of creating sustainable development for these areas.

Exercise 5.16

Text 5.18 was written by a student in Year 3 as part of a unit of work on spiders. Read the text and answer the questions to help you assess the outcomes achieved by the student.

Text 5.18

I think spiders should not be killed unless they are dangerous. Don't you know that spiders kill flies and mosquitos and make nice webs in the garden? They do not hurt people unless people interfere with them. Would you like to be killed when you weren't hurting anybody? Do you think that would be fair? No, it wouldn't! So please don't kill spiders!

Jenny (Age 7)

i. What is the writer trying to achieve?

....

ii. How has the student structured or staged the text?

....

....

....

iii. Describe the types of clauses the student has used to interact with the reader.

....

iv. Do you think the writer's way of interacting with the reader helps her to achieve her purpose?

....

v. Where would you place the interaction in the text on the following cline?

Impersonal   Personal

<--->

Formal   Informal

vi. What advice would you give the student to help her to interact with the reader in a more impersonal and formal way?

....

....

....

Exercise 5.17

Text 5.19 was written by a student during a unit focussing on issues in the local community. The teacher asked students to write a letter of complaint about an issue which affected them.

Text 5.19

Dear Mr Jones,

I am writing to complain about your dog's barking. The barking is so loud that I am completely unable to hear my television. The dog always keeps me awake every night. I must have my sleep, otherwise I am unable to do my schoolwork the next day.

Please keep your dog quiet. Either lock it inside the house or in the garage.

Yours sincerely

Amy Johnston

i. Comment on the interpersonal resources the writer has used to persuade the reader to take action to stop his dog from barking.

....

....

....

ii. Use the resources of modality to temper some of the judgments and recommendations in Text 5.19. This may involve the use of modal verbs, adverbs, adjectives, nouns or indirect expressions of modality. It may also involve lowering the degree of modality which has been used. An example of a clause which has been tempered is provided.

Clauses from Text 5.19	Tempered version
I am completely unable to hear my television.	I am often unable to hear my television.
The dog always keeps me awake every night.	
I must have my sleep,	
Please keep your dog quiet.	
Either lock it inside the house or in the garage.	

Exercise 5.18

Use the following table to record your understanding of the key terms introduced in this chapter.

Term	Your understanding of the term
Lexis	
Imperative clause	
Declarative clause	
Interrogative clause	
Modality	
Interpersonal metaphor	
Attitude	
Affect	
Judgement	
Appreciation	
Graduation	

6 Creating well organised and cohesive texts

Another important function of language is to weave meanings into a coherent and cohesive whole. The way we use language to organise the information in a text and to make connections across a text is known as the **textual** function of language. There are a number of important grammatical resources that help make something a 'text' rather than a random collection of clauses or sentences. These textual resources are concerned with:

- The organisation of information and ideas at both text and clause level

- The different types of cohesive links and connections that can be made across a text.

The way in which language weaves meanings into text is greatly influenced by features of the context in which the text occurs, particularly the social purpose and the channel of communication. For example, different text types and different 'modes' of communication (ie. CD ROM, telephone conversation, lecture, postcard, medical textbook) will draw upon the text-creating resources in different ways.

In this chapter we will look at three important resources for organisation—the use of **text** and **paragraph previews**, **theme** and **nominalisation**. We will then consider some of the resources that make connections across a text, those to do with **cohesion**.

6.1 Organising ideas

Text and paragraph previews

Unlike spontaneous casual conversation, many spoken and written texts need some degree of planning and organisation. This is particularly important in longer written texts, where information needs to be organised into paragraphs. In these texts, it is extremely important to provide clear signals to the audience about where the text is headed and how the information will be organised.

Exercise 6.1

Read Text 6.1 and answer the questions that follow.

Text 6.1

Trail bikes in National Parks have become a huge problem for park rangers and there are many reasons why they should be totally banned.

The first reason is that trail bikes cause lots of damage to the native plants in the area. Riders make tracks through the bush and destroy many of the plants and trees. The tracks are used again and again which makes it hard for the plants to grow back. This also causes severe soil erosion.

The second reason is the noise from the trail bikes. This noise is very annoying and spoils the peace and quiet of the park for visitors. It also scares many of the native animals away from their natural environment.

Another reason is the danger of riding in National Parks. Many riders go to isolated and rugged parts of the park. This increases the risk of an injury and means that riders are a long way from help if they have an accident.

All visitors to National Parks should do their best to protect the natural environment for everyone to enjoy. Therefore trail bikes should be totally banned and there should be severe fines for anyone who is caught.

i. What is the purpose of Text 6.1?

....

....

....

ii. How does the writer help the reader make an initial prediction about the way in which the whole text will develop?

....

....

....

iii. How does the writer signal the content of each paragraph?

....

....

....

iv. How do these 'signals' help organise the writer's argument?

....

....

....

....

As you can see, the writer of Text 6.1 has used paragraphs to organise the information into groups of related points (in this case 'reasons'). These are predicted in the introduction by the clause *and there are many reasons why they should be totally banned.* This is called a **text preview**. A text preview signals a particular kind of organisation and helps the reader make a prediction about how the text will develop.

The reader of Text 6.1 is further guided through the text by the use of **paragraph previews** (often referred to as topic sentences). These occur at the beginning of each paragraph and signal its content. Each paragraph preview also makes a clear link back to the text preview, contributing to the overall coherence. This is shown on Text 6.1 below.

Text 6.1

Trail bikes in National Parks have become a huge problem for park rangers and there are many reasons why they should be totally banned. .... text preview

paragraph preview .. The first reason is that trail bikes cause lots of damage to the native plants in the area. Riders make tracks through the bush and destroy many of the plants and trees. The tracks are used again and again which makes it hard for the plants to grow back. This also causes severe soil erosion.

paragraph preview .. The second reason is the noise from the trail bikes. This noise is very annoying and spoils the peace and quiet of the park for visitors. It also scares many of the native animals away from their natural environment.

Another reason is the danger of riding in National Parks. .... paragraph preview
Many riders go to isolated and rugged parts of the park. This increases the risk of an injury and means that riders are a long way from help if they have an accident.

All visitors to National Parks should do their best to protect the natural environment for everyone to enjoy. Therefore trail bikes should be totally banned and there should be severe fines for anyone who is caught.

Text and paragraph previews are a crucial aspect of organisation in longer texts. As well as helping writers with organisation, text and paragraph previews help readers locate information and assist with important reading strategies such as skimming and scanning.

Exercise 6.2

Read Text 6.2 and highlight any text and paragraph previews. Then answer the questions below.

Text 6.2

Many species of animals are threatened with extinction because of the way people change the land. The main threats to animals are loss of habitat, introduced animals and hunting.

Loss of habitat

Loss of habitat has already led to the extinction of many species of animals. When people clear land for housing and roads, there is no longer enough space and food for the animals living in the area. This kind of development also increases the amount of pollution which harms animals and their habitats.

Introduced animals

Introduced animals are those that are brought to an area where they do not naturally live. Many introduced animals, such as cats, foxes and rabbits, threaten the survival of native animals. For example, in Australia, foxes and cats hunt native animals, and rabbits eat the plants the native animals feed on.

Hunting

Many animals are hunted by people. Some are killed for their meat, fur and body parts. Others are hunted for sport or for trophies and souvenirs. Some of the biggest animals in the world, such as whales and elephants, have almost been hunted to extinction.

i. What is the purpose and text type of Text 6.2?

....

....

....

ii. Why do you think the writer has included a sub-heading as part of each paragraph preview?

....

....

....

iii. Is there a relationship between the order of the points in the text preview and their order in the body of the text? Why is this important?

....

....

....

....

Exercise 6.3

Read the following information report about clowns. How might you use a text preview and paragraph previews to organise the information into paragraphs? Rewrite the text in the space provided. You may change some of the wording if necessary.

Text 6.3

Whiteface clowns cover their face with white make-up and do a lot of physical stunts like leaping and tumbling. They evolved from the theatrical entertainers of earlier times. Auguste clowns wear colourful, ill fitting clothing and oversized shoes. They also have bulbous noses and brightly coloured wigs. These clowns became popular during the nineteenth century. Character clowns make fun of the human condition and may impersonate characters such as a cowboy, fireman, tramp or policeman. The more recent "New Vaudeville" clowns involve the audience in the performance. Mime, juggling, acrobatics, magic tricks and traditional clowning may be part of their act.

Source: *Here Come the Clowns* (Swortzell:1978)

Rewrite Text 6.3 here:

....

....

....

....

....

....

....

....

....

....

....

....

....

....

....

Theme

Text and paragraph previews are part of a much bigger system of organisation called **theme**. Theme can be described as the 'starting point' for a text, paragraph or clause.

Theme operates at a variety of levels and plays an important role in orienting readers (and listeners) to how the topic is being developed. For example, text previews function as the starting point or theme of a whole text, and orient the reader to the paragraph previews that are likely to follow. Similarly, paragraph previews function as the starting point or theme of a paragraph, and orient readers to the point or topic that is going to be developed in that paragraph.

Individual clauses also have a starting point or theme. The choice and patterning of clause level themes across a paragraph or text help organise meaning and structure text in different ways.

Exercise 6.4
Read Text 6.4 and 6.5 and answer the questions below.

Text 6.4
Dawn Fraser is an Australian swimming legend. She was born in 1937 in Balmain, Sydney. As a young child, Dawn had asthma and began swimming because it helped her breathing. During her teens, she trained with coach Harry Gallagher and in 1956 qualified for the Melbourne Olympics, where she won her first gold medal. After that, Dawn became a permanent member of the Australian Swimming Team. In 1962, Dawn became the first woman to swim 100 metres in less than a minute. After the Tokyo Olympics in 1964, Dawn was banned from competition for ten years for something she didn't do. This caused her early retirement from swimming. Since then she has become a celebrity, running a pub in Balmain and more recently, taking an active role in politics.

Source: http://www.abc.net.au/btn/australians/fraser.htm

i. What is the text about?

....

....

ii. How would you describe the purpose of the text?

....

....

iii. What do you notice about the starting point of many of the clauses?

....

....

....

Text 6.5
Kangaroos are Australia's largest marsupial. Their scientific name is Macropus rufus. Kangaroos live in open forests and grasslands. They like to shelter from the sun under shady trees. Kangaroos have 2 small front feet which are like hands. They use these to scratch themselves and hold food. They have much bigger hind legs for hopping. Some kangaroos can leap 8 metres in a single bound. Kangaroos can move as fast as 40-50 km per hour.

Fatima (Age 8)

i. What is the text about?

....

ii. How would you describe the purpose of the text?

....

....

iii. What do you notice about the starting point of many of the clauses?

....

....

....

Text 6.4 is a biographical recount of a famous Olympian, Dawn Fraser. In texts such as this, it is important to give clear signals about the unfolding of events in time. Text 6.5 is a report about kangaroos, giving information about their appearance, habitat and behaviour. The theme choices in each text are quite different and contribute to the overall sense of what each text is 'about'. In Text 6.4, we find that many of the clauses begin with adverbials to do with time. In Text 6.5, the clauses mostly begin with noun groups (or pronouns) that refer to kangaroos, thus keeping the topic in focus.

Exercise 6.5

Identify the clause themes in Texts 6.4 and 6.5. In Text 6.4, highlight any adverbials of time that appear near the beginning of a clause. In Text 6.5, highlight any noun groups or pronouns referring to kangaroos that appear at the beginning of a clause.

As the previous examples have shown, we can make choices about how we start a clause or sentence. The theme of a clause can be expressed by different grammatical elements, depending on the purpose of the text and its focus.

There are three main types of theme: themes that foreground experiential meaning, themes that foreground interpersonal meaning and themes that highlight relationships between parts of text. Let's look at each of these in turn.

Experiential themes

One of the major functions of theme is to establish and maintain a clear focus on the topic or content; in other words some aspect of experiential meaning. This focus will vary according to whether the theme is a noun group, a verb or an adverbial.

When we start a clause with a noun group, it highlights the names of the *people*, *places*, *things* or *concepts* that we want to be the focus. This is a very common type of theme because so many text types consist of statements only. For example:

The moon is a natural satellite. *A satellite* is an object in space that orbits a bigger object such as a planet. *Our moon* orbits the planet Earth. *It* is a sphere and has lots of craters and mountains. *The moon* has no oxygen or water.

Sometimes however, we use a verb to start a clause and the clause takes on the form of a command. In these clauses, the starting point is the specific action or behaviour that is important to achieving a goal. For example:

1. **Count** your spots and **join** them with a pen to make pictures.
2. **Carve** one of your bed posts into a totem pole.
3. **Draw** different kinds of insects on your toenails with coloured felt pens.
4. **Dip** tissues into your glass of water and mould them into little animals.

Adapted from *Robin Klein's Crookbook* (Klein 1987:8-9)

Alternatively, we may choose to start a clause with an adverbial, foregrounding the circumstances relating to the topic, such as time, manner, place etc. For example:

Last weekend my friend Callum came over to play. We played soccer all morning and I scored the most goals. **After morning tea** we went over to the creek to catch yabbies. We caught three little ones and put them in a bucket. **On the way back** some of the cows in the paddock started to chase us.

Exercise 6.6

Many texts contain a variety of experiential themes. Highlight and label the different types of experiential themes in the extract below.

Fill a jar half full with water. Pour some cooking oil on top. Put the lid on and shake. After a few minutes, the oil floats back to the top. Oil is a liquid that won't dissolve in water. Water is also heavier and it sinks to the bottom.

Experiential themes such as these are sometimes preceeded by a comment adverbial (ie. an interpersonal theme) or a text connective (ie. a textual theme). Let's look at how these combine with the experiential theme to give the clause a particular kind of orientation.

Interpersonal themes

It is possible to give a clause an interpersonal orientation by placing a comment adverbial before the experiential theme. Comment adverbials used in this way are called *interpersonal themes* because they foreground the position of the writer or speaker. It is important to note that comment adverbials do not always come at the beginning of a clause. However, placing them at the beginning draws attention to the writer's attitude towards the topic or their assessment of a situation. For example (interpersonal theme in **bold**; experiential theme underlined):

Surprisingly, Brown's new stage production has opened to full houses. **In my opinion**, this long awaited musical comedy is gutless. I much preferred the film version.

On the way back some of the cows in the paddock started to chase us. **Quite frankly**, I thought we were in big trouble! **Thankfully**, we made it to the gate in time.

Textual themes

We can also use the beginning of a clause to signal relationships between ideas and make the connections between parts of a text explicit. These are called *textual themes* and also come before the experiential theme. The two types of textual theme are text connectives and conjunctions. Textual themes may express relationships to do with cause/effect, time and sequence, condition, concession etc.[1]

Text connectives help structure a text by linking sentences and paragraphs in a logical way. Again, they do not always come at the beginning of a sentence. But by placing them first we signal that the logical relationship is something we want readers to pay attention to. For example (text connectives in **bold**; experiential themes underlined):

> Trail bikes are becoming a real problem in our National Parks. They damage many of the native plants in the area and cause soil erosion. ***As a result***, the natural habitat of many native animals is destroyed. ***Moreover***, the noise from trail bikes spoils the peace and quiet of the park for visitors. ***Therefore*** trail bikes should be banned from these areas.

Conjunctions join clauses within a sentence and always appear at the beginning of the clause. They tell us how one clause is linked to another by expressing the relationship between ideas. For example (conjunctions in **bold**; experiential themes underlined):

> It is important to visit the dentist ***because*** she helps look after your teeth. The dentist usually cleans your teeth ***when*** you go for a check-up ***but*** sometimes she might give you a filling. The dentist will give you braces ***if*** your teeth are crooked.

Another theme choice that plays an important role in the organisation of meaning is the position of the dependent clause in a complex sentence. Note the difference between Example 1 and 2 below (Dependent clauses are in *italics* with the linking conjunction in **bold**).

Example 1
One plate is forced underneath the other ***when*** *the two plates collide*. It heats up ***because*** *the plate moves downwards*. This heating creates magma. The magma bursts through the crust ***as*** *the heat and pressure continue to build up*.

Example 2
When *the two plates collide*, one plate is forced underneath the other. ***Because*** *the plate moves downwards*, it heats up. This heating creates magma. ***As*** *the heat and pressure continue to build up*, the magma bursts through the crust.

In Example 2, the dependent clauses (ie. the clauses starting with a conjunction) have been put *first* in the sentence. This has the effect of highlighting or *thematising* the relationship between the clauses. Explanations draw heavily on this kind of pattern because it allows the writer to link events and foreground reasons, consequences and steps in a process.

[1] See Derewianka (1998:110-111) for further examples of conjunctions and text connectives.

Exercise 6.7

Read Text 6.6 and answer the questions below. The text has been divided into clauses, with each clause on a new line. The themes are in **bold**.

Text 6. 6

Make a decorative jar of stones

Firstly, collect some stones with interesting shapes, textures and colours.

Put them in a bowl of warm soapy water

and scrub them with a brush.

Then rinse the stones

and stand them on a window sill for a day.

Next, give the stones a thin coat of varnish.

Let the varnish dry.

Finally, arrange the stones in a glass jar or container

and use it as an ornament.

i. What is the purpose and text type of Text 6.6?

....
....

ii. Circle the text connectives and underline the conjunctions. Why are these types of textual themes important in procedures?

....
....
....
....

iii. Highlight the experiential theme of each clause. How do they contribute to the overall purpose of the text?

....
....
....
....

Exercise 6.8

Figure 6.1 is of the water cycle. Write an explanation of the water cycle, remembering to use the stages of an explanation as described in the Appendix. Pay attention to how you use themes to move the reader through the stages in the cycle. Write your completed explanation in the space provided. Compare your text with others and discuss the similarities and differences.

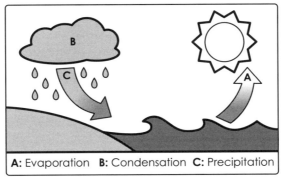

A: Evaporation **B:** Condensation **C:** Precipitation

Figure 6.1

Write your completed explanation here:

....

....

....

....

....

....

Exercise 6.9

Write a report comparing the Northern Territory and Tasmania using the information in the table below. Consider how you might use text and paragraph previews as well as clause themes to help structure the text. Write your completed report in the space provided. Compare your text with others and discuss the similarities and differences.

	Northern Territory	Tasmania
General description and location	Largest territory; located in the mid-north; capital Darwin; population 169,000; north of the territory is tropical, south is arid desert	Smallest & southernmost island state; capital Hobart; population 472,000; one of a group of 300 small islands
Climate	Tropical north has two distinct seasons—wet and dry; wet season brings high humidity, tropical storms, cyclones	Mild temperate maritime climate; snow in alpine areas; highest average rainfall in Australia
Geography	Coast—swamps, mudflats, mangroves; north east—Kakadu National Park, Katherine Gorge; south—desert, arid plains, Uluru (Ayers Rock)	More than half is a World Heritage Area; extensive areas of mountain terrain; alpine heathland; ancient Huon pine forests; pockets of remote untouched rainforest in southeast
Fauna	North—freshwater and saltwater crocodiles, deadly box jelly-fish, water birds (jabiru & magpie geese); desert—dingo, bilby	Tasmanian devil; Tasmanian tiger (now extinct); migrating whales; eastern quoll

Write your completed report here:

....

....

....

....

....

....

....

....

....

....

....

....

....

....

....

....

....

....

....

....

....

....

....

Another way of changing the theme of a clause is to 'shift emphasis' by choosing either the **active** or the **passive** form of the verb. If a clause is active, the person or thing *doing* the action comes first in the clause. If a clause is passive, the person or thing *affected* by the action comes first. For example:

Active: **Soldiers** destroyed the entire village.
Passive: **The entire village** was destroyed by soldiers.

Active: **Early settlers** cleared large areas of rainforest for industrial use.
Passive: **Large areas of rainforest** were cleared for industrial use.

We use the active form when we want to focus on the person or thing doing the action (ie. the 'responsible' participant). We use the passive form when we want to focus on the person or thing affected by the action. The passive also allows us to 'ignore' and leave out the responsible participant altogether. For example, *The entire village was destroyed*. For this reason, the passive is often a feature of historical and bureaucratic discourse and news stories.

Patterns of theme choice across texts

The patterning of themes across a text help make the text more predictable. We have already seen a number of possible patterns; for example the repeated use of time adverbials in Text 6.4, the noun groups focusing on kangaroos in Text 6.5 and the textual themes and commands in Text 6.6.

The basic principle underlying these patterns and contributing to the 'predictablity' of text is that theme choices should not be 'unexpected'—they should be connected with ideas presented in previous clauses. In other words, the theme is our 'known' starting point and 'new' information about the topic is built up in the rest of the clause. For example:

Theme	New information
Water	is an integral part of life on this planet.
It	is an odourless, tasteless substance that covers more than three quarters of the earths surface.
Most of the water on earth	is salt water found in the oceans.
Two percent of the earth's water	is in solid form in ice-caps and glaciers
and only one percent	is in a form useable to humans and land animals.
This fresh water	is found in lakes, rivers, streams, ponds and in the ground.

Another pattern that is commonly used in sequences of clauses is a 'zig-zag' pattern. This occurs when an element that is first introduced as new information then becomes the theme of a following clause, and so on. For example:

Theme	New information
A cold front	begins when cold air moves into an area which has warmer air.
The warmer air	rises over the heavier cold air.
As this	occurs,
The warm air	cools and condenses into water droplets.
These droplets	join to form form larger heavier droplets
and then the droplets	fall as rain.

A third pattern occurs when new information gets 'split up' or divided into parts that can then be used for the themes of subsequent clauses. This often occurs when the writer wants to introduce a number of points or sub-points. For example:

Theme	New information
The water cycle	is made up of **three main processes**.
These processes	are **evaporation**, **condensation** and **precipitation**.
Evaporation	occurs when the sun heats up the water
and	turns it into vapour or steam.
The water vapour	then goes into the air.
Condensation	occurs when the vapour in the air gets cold
and	changes back into liquid (or water droplets), forming clouds.
Precipitation	occurs when the clouds get heavy
and water	falls back to the Earth in the form of rain, hail, sleet or snow.

It is important to note that these patterns are *resources* for organising text and as such should not be seen as 'fixed'. Again, writers draw upon these patterns across paragraphs and texts according to their purpose. Paragraphs may follow one pattern throughout or combine several. A pattern may also be interrupted in order to highlight certain information, or to signal a new stage in the text.

Narratives use themes in many different ways. In the orientation stage of a narrative, the themes may focus on the main character, as the writer builds up a description. The themes may also be adverbials that help set the story in time and place. In the complication and resolution stages however, the themes may be totally *unpredictable*. This helps build suspense and adds to the element of surprise—you don't know what will happen next. Try making predictions about how this paragraph will develop! (Themes in **bold**)

Sophie crouched as still as a mouse inside the BFG's pocket. **She** hardly dared breathe. **The slightest sound or movement** would give her away. **Through the tiny peep-hole** she watched the giants clustering around the poor BFG. **How revolting** they were! **All of them** had piggy little eyes and enormous mouths with thick sausage lips. *When the Fleshlumpeater* was speaking, **she** got a glimpse of his tongue. **It** was jet black, like a slab of black steak.

Source: *The BFG* (Dahl 1982:73)

Nominalisation: moving towards abstraction

In this section we look at another important textual resource—**nominalisation**. Nominalisation refers to the process of turning words that are not normally nouns (ie. verbs, conjunctions, adjectives, and adverbs) into nouns; for example, employ (verb) ⟶ employment (noun).

Nominalisation is an important resource for creating abstract and technical terms and for condensing information in texts. Nominalisation is also one of the major differences between spoken and written language.

Let's compare the following texts to illustrate some of these differences.

Exercise 6.10

Read Texts 6.7 and 6.8 and answer the questions below.

Text 6.7

When people clear land for houses and roads they change the environment. They destroy the forest and bushland and then many animals lose their homes. More houses and roads will pollute the environment even more. Some animals have become extinct because their homes have been destroyed.

Text 6.8

Clearing and development of land often results in the destruction of the natural habitat of many local species. It may also increase the level of pollution. Loss of habitat has already led to the extinction of many species of animals.

i. What do you see as the main differences between these texts?

....

....

....

....

....

ii. Which text do you think would be more highly 'valued' as students move through school? Why?

....

....

....

....

The main difference between Text 6.7 and Text 6.8 is the use of nominalisation. Text 6.7 uses everyday language to describe the actions of people and the impact this has on the environment. Text 6.8 uses nominalisation to name causes and effects (eg. *destruction, pollution, loss, extinction*) in an abstract way. Nominalisation becomes increasingly important as students move through primary school into secondary school. Textbooks and other resources used in specialised subjects such as history, science, maths and geography use nominalisation to package more information into sentences and increasingly, students are expected to use nominalisation to demonstrate that they understand the more abstract concepts in these subjects.

Identifying and forming nominalisations

Nominalisations can be formed in a variety of ways. These are described in Table 6.1.

Table 6.1: How nominalisations are formed

From verb to noun
Many verbs can be changed into nouns
a. by changing the ending of the verb form:
discuss ⟶ discussion; identify ⟶ identity; arrange ⟶ arrangement
b. by using the form verb+ing: her acting, an old saying
Some verbs can be used as nouns without any change eg. the cause, a visit, a struggle.
From conjunction to noun
Nouns can also be used to represent relationships typically expressed by conjunctions:
a. Expressing cause:
The customer left **because** *the food was cold*. (conjunction)
The customer's **reason** for leaving was the cold soup. (noun)
b. Expressing comparison:
Roebourne is a small town **whereas** *Karratha is large*. (conjunction)
One **difference** between Roebourne and Karratha is their size. (noun)
From adjective to noun
Adjectives can also be nominalised and turned into a noun form. For example:
expensive ⟶ expense; unstable ⟶ instability; tense ⟶ tension
From clause to nominal group
Noun groups containing nominalisations are often used to condense meanings that would otherwise be spread across a number of clauses. For example:
a. I am going to develop my ideas in a logical way because that helps me structure my essay.
b. The logical **development** of ideas contributes to the **structure** of an essay.

Texts that use a lot of nominalisation often appear very dense and can be difficult to read. This is because nominalisation changes how we 'package' information in a clause. These changes include:

- Noun groups that name abstract phenomenon such as ideas, causes, reasons etc.

- Noun groups that are more complex

- Use of relating verbs (including those to do with cause and effect) to link the noun groups

- Information often condensed to a simple sentence with one clause

- The removal of 'actors' ie. those responsible for action, evidence or arguments.

Exercise 6.11

Let's look again at Texts 6.7 and 6.8. Complete the tables below to compare some of the grammatical features of these texts.

Text 6.7

When people clear land for houses and roads they change the environment. They destroy the forest and bushland and then many animals lose their homes. More houses and roads will pollute the environment even more. Some animals have become extinct because their homes have been destroyed.

Text 6.8

Clearing and development of land often results in the destruction of the natural habitat of many local species. It may also increase the level of pollution. Loss of habitat has already led to the extinction of many species of animals.

Grammatical features of Text 6.7	Examples
Complex and compound sentences	
Simple noun groups about people, concrete things	
Clauses with action verbs and human 'actors'	
Conjunctions expressing cause/effect between clauses	

Grammatical features of Text 6.8	Examples
Simple sentences	
Longer noun groups about abstract things	
Clauses with relating verbs expressing cause/effect; no human 'actors'	

One of the effects of nominalisation is that it condenses meaning into the noun groups in a clause. Once something has been turned into a noun or *nominalised*, it then becomes possible to use adjectivals to further describe, classify, evaluate or measure it. Table 6.2 describes resources for building noun groups around nominalisations.

Table 6.2: Modifying a nominalisation

a. **Classifiers** can help define the main noun by specifying type or subject area:
eg. *medical* facilities; *physical* isolation; *political* unrest; *economic* rationalism
Many of these are also abstractions.

b. **Adjectivals** often indicate importance or significance:
eg. *complex* internal relationships; *widespread* political unrest
They can also intensify ie. *extremely* complex internal relationships

c. **Adjectivals** may help generalise about quantity/extent:
eg. *additional* medical facilities; *several* contributing factors; *many* important reasons

d. **Adjectival phrases** help with the meaning of the abstract term and are often a vital part of these noun groups. These may also include nominalisations:

eg. A rapid increase *in the <u>rate</u> of population <u>growth</u>* ...
      The inconvenience and expense of <u>participation</u> *in programs such as this* ...

Exercise 6.12

Use nominalisation to rewrite the following examples. Try to compact the meaning into a *simple sentence*. To do this you will need to form a noun group around a nominalisation and then think about how the noun groups *relate* to each other in order to complete the sentence. You may want to refer back to Table 6.1 and 6.2. Write your more abstract, condensed version in the space provided.

Example:

Original: When people plant a lot of crops year after year, many of the nutrients go out of the soil.

Rewritten: *Overcropping often causes a breakdown in the soil.*

i. Over the last couple of years, people from all over the world have been arguing about whether or not the hole in the ozone layer has been getting bigger.

....

....

ii. Many people live in urban areas but if the population gets too high the city will get really polluted and there mightn't be enough houses for people to live in.

....

....

Exercise 6.13

It is also important to be able to 'unpack' the meaning in abstract noun groups when you encounter them in reading. The noun groups in the following example are in bold. Highlight the nominalisations in each noun group. Unpack this example as if you had to explain it to someone without using the nominalisations. Note how many sentences it takes to get the same information across.

The unlawful killing of sharks is **an important marine-conservation issue. A decline in shark numbers** may lead to **the extinction of some species**.

....

....

....

....

....

....

....

....

....

....

Nominalisation and text types

Nominalisation is a key feature of the more specialised and abstract written texts that students begin to encounter as they move through school. Nominalisation allows us to name abstract ideas, arguments, reasons, causes etc. and is an important resource for the successful development of many factual text types.

For example, it is through nominalisation that we are able to introduce technical terms in explanations and reports. Nominalisation allows us to sum up an explanation sequence or process using a single technical term. This is illustrated in the following examples:

> Heat from the sun causes liquid water to become water vapour. This process is called **evaporation**.

> An increase in the number of people moving to urban areas has led to a housing shortage in the inner city. **Urbanisation** has also placed increasing demands on services such as education and transport.

Nominalisation also helps writers 'get their themes right'. Many theme patterns rely on nominalisation to condense previous information into a single word that can then be used to move the text along. For example:

> When the sun heats up the water, it evaporates into steam. **Evaporation** causes the steam to rise into the air. When the water vapour in the air gets cold, it condenses into water droplets and forms clouds. When the clouds get heavy, these droplets fall to the ground. This is called **precipitation**. **Precipitation** may be in the form of rain, hail, sleet or snow.

As students begin to write longer texts, nominalisation helps with organisation and structure by allowing writers to develop a clear framework for headings and text and paragraph previews. This framework becomes a very useful guide for reading, research and note-taking.

For example, in reports this may involve naming abstract categories for descriptions. A report on a city might include descriptions about location, tourist attractions, population and transport. A report comparing the different levels of government could focus on organisational structure, responsibilities and legislation. In explanations nominalisation names causes, effects and consequences. In expositions and discussions, nominalisation allows us to name arguments, reasons, factors, issues etc.

6.2 Cohesion: making connections

The grammatical resources which writers and speakers use to link information and make connections across a text are collectively known as **cohesion**. Cohesion refers to the way in which a text 'hangs together'; to the resources within language that help relate ideas and information and make links between different parts of a text. There are five different cohesive resources—**reference**, **ellipsis**, **substitution**, **lexical cohesion** and **text connectives**. We will look at each of these in turn.

Reference

Referring words are those that 'point' to something in a text. They make links by referring back to something previously mentioned in the text or by pointing forward to something further on. In written language, referring words can also point to a section of co-text or to other locations outside the text such as illustrations, diagrams, tables and graphs. In spoken language, referring words often point to something in the shared physical context.

The main referring words are listed in Table 6.3.

Table 6.3: Examples of referring words

Personal pronouns	I/me/mine/my we/us/ours/our he/him/his it/its	you/yours/your they/them/theirs/their she/her/hers
Demonstratives	Definite article: the Pronouns: this, these, that, those Adverbs: here, now, there, then	
Comparatives	Same/different, other, bigger/est (etc.), more/less	

Text 6.9 is a segment of mother/child interaction. The referring words have been highlighted.

Text 6.9

M: Susie, **here**'s your apple.

S: Yuk! **That** piece has got a brown spot on **it**. I want a **different** one!

M: Susie, **the** apple's fine... stop fussing.

S: **It**'s not fair. James hasn't got any brown pieces. **His** are nice.

M: Well, put **that** piece **there** and eat the **others**.

S: Don't want **them** either! Can I have a banana instead?

The kind of reference found in Text 6.9 is typical of spoken language, where many of the referring words point *outside* the text itself—to objects and behaviours in the physical context, and to experiences and understandings that are shared and 'understood' by the speakers. As a result, it is difficult to retrieve the meaning of referring words like *that*, *there* and *them* unless you are actually part of the context.

Exercise 6.14

Highlight the referring words in Text 6.10 (this extract accompanies a labelled diagram). Note the kind of reference that is used. How does it differ from Text 6.10?

Text 6.10

The oesophagus lies beneath the trachea inside the chest. It runs behind the lungs and heart. This is the view down the inside of the oesophagus. Beneath its mucus-covered lining there are muscles that run down the length of the oesophagus and in a circular pattern around it. These muscles take over from the throat muscles after food is swallowed. They work together to squeeze the softened food down towards the stomach. This is the next stop on our journey.

Source: *The Human Body* (Harris 2000:11)

As you can see, most of the reference in this text points back to words in the text itself. Pronouns refer back to noun groups in the text and the definite article *the* is used to refer to things that are assumed to be part of our general knowledge of the topic. Reference of this kind is common in written language and is often used to avoid repetition. However, too much reference can also sound repetitive and reference that is inconsistent in gender or number can make a text difficult to follow.

Ellipsis and substitution

As a text unfolds, it is not always necessary to explicitly mention every component again and again. To avoid repetition, we sometimes leave out components of a clause or replace them with a shorter, substitute word. Omitting a component of a clause is called **ellipsis**. Replacing a component of a clause with a shorter word like *one, some, do* is called **substitution**. The following extract includes several instances of both ellipsis (in brackets) and substitution (in **bold**).

Text 6.11

R: Hi Sue... yeh, things are still pretty bad here.

S: What can you see from where you are now?

R: Well, (*I can see*) lots of ash and the occasional eruption from the volcano.

S: Has there been **one** recently?

R: The last (*eruption*) was about an hour ago. But they're expecting more (*eruptions*) as the night goes on.

S: Has there been much talk of evacuation?

R: Yes, there was **some** earlier today, but they haven't made any decisions yet.

S: Well let us know when they **do**.

Again, both ellipsis and substitution are common in spoken texts, where much of what is being said can be taken for granted and need not be repeated in every turn. In written language however, they need to be used sparingly. It can be very tiresome for the reader if they have to constantly 'replace' ellipsis and substitution in a written text.

Lexical cohesion

Cohesion can also be achieved through different kinds of word associations or semantic relationships between the vocabulary or *lexical items* in a text. This is called **lexical cohesion**. Different kinds of lexical cohesion are illustrated in the analysis of Text 6.12 below (see Table 6.4).

Text 6.12

Wombats are Australia's largest burrowing marsupial. There are two types of wombat, the Common Wombat and the Hairy-Nosed Wombat.

The Common Wombat has coarse fur and no hair on its nose. Their body is 1.1 metres long and they have a short tail. In comparison, the Hairy-Nosed Wombat has soft, silky fur and white hair on its nose. They have a slightly smaller body and a longer tail. All wombats have short legs and very sharp claws for digging.

Wombats live only in south-east Australia. The Common Wombat lives in forests and woodlands, whereas the Hairy-Nosed Wombat lives in open scrub and grasslands.

Wombats are nocturnal. They sleep in their burrows during the day and come out to feed at night. Wombats are also herbivores which means that they are plant-eaters.

Table 6.4

Type of lexical cohesion	Examples from Text 6.12
The use of **synonyms** ie. words that are similar in meaning.	Herbivores/plant-eaters
The use of **antonyms** ie. words that that have opposite or contrastive meanings.	Long/short; coarse fur/soft, silky fur; woodlands/grasslands; day/night;
The use of **repetition** ie. words that are repeated across a text.	Wombats; the Common Wombat; the Hairy-Nosed Wombat;
The use of **collocation** ie. words that co-occur because they share a common element of meaning.	Sleep/day/feed/night
Words that form a **class/sub-class** relationship.	• Burrowing marsupial/wombat • Wombat—Common/Hairy-Nosed • Nocturnal/wombat • Herbivore/wombat
Words that form a **whole/part** relationship.	• Body—fur/nose/tail/legs/claws • South-east Australia—forests/woodlands/open scrub/grasslands

The lexical items in a text form 'sets' of words that are associated in different ways. Given that this text is a report, it's not surprising that many words are associated by class/sub-class and whole/part relationships. The comparison of the two types of wombats also uses antonyms, while repetition of the themes helps maintain the focus on wombats.

Exercise 6.15
Read Text 6.13 and using a highlighter, mark any examples of lexical cohesion. Then record them in the table that follows.

Text 6.13
I believe that junk food should not be sold in the school canteen for the following reasons. The main reason is that junk food is bad for your health. Unhealthy foods like chocolate bars, ice-creams, coke and sweets are full of sugar, fat and food colouring. Another reason is that it creates more rubbish in the playground because of all the packets and wrappers. Also, if students buy junk food their behaviour may be affected by all the sugar and chemicals. However, if they bought healthy foods they would have lots of energy and brainpower.

Type of lexical cohesion	Examples from Text 6.13
The use of **synonyms** ie. words that are similar in meaning.	
The use of **antonyms** ie. words that that have opposite or contrastive meanings.	
The use of **repetition** ie. words that are repeated across a text.	
The use of **collocation** ie. words that co-occur because they share a common element of meaning.	
Words that form a **class/sub-class** relationship.	
Words that form a **whole/part** relationship.	

Text connectives

Another set of resources for holding a text together are **text connectives**. Text connectives make the development or sequence of ideas explicit for the reader, by providing signals about the logical relationships that exist between the sentences and paragraphs in a text. Text connectives are often, but not always, found at the beginning of sentences.

Text connectives link parts of a text in many different ways. Derewianka (1998) lists six important functions of text connectives. These are illustrated in Table 6.5.

Table 6.5: Types of text connectives

Clarifying		Showing cause/result	
In other words	in particular	so	as a result
For example	in fact	then	for that reason
for instance	that is	therefore	due to
to be more precise	to illustrate	as a consequence/ consequently	accordingly because of this
Indicating time		**Sequencing ideas**	
Then	next	Firstly/first of all	briefly
afterwards	at the same time	to start with/to begin,	finally/a final point
in the end	finally	second, third, fourth ...	in conclusion
soon	after a while	at this point	given the above points
later	previously	to summarise/sum up	
until then			
Adding information		**Condition/Concession**	
In addition	also	In that case	on the other hand
furthermore	as well	otherwise	on the contrary
moreover	and besides	however	anyhow/anyway
similarly/equally	along with	nevertheless	even so
in the same way	above all	despite this	at least
		besides	though
		yet	

Source: Derewianka, B. (1998) *A Grammar Companion for Primary Teachers,* Primary English Teaching Association, Sydney

Text connectives perform a different job to conjunctions. As we saw in Chapter 3 (and earlier in this chapter), conjunctions join clauses together to form compound and complex sentences. Text connectives however, function at the text level, linking sentences or paragraphs.

6.3 **Bringing it all together**

Writers and speakers draw upon the resources of theme, nominalisation and cohesion in different ways depending on their purpose, the subject matter and the channel of communication. These grammatical resources are important features of the longer, more specialised texts that students are expected to read and produce as they move through school.

Exercise 6.16

This student writer demonstrates good control over many of the resources for organisation and cohesion. Read Text 6.14 and answer the questions below.

Text 6.14

Cities

Cities are large towns that have many kinds of buildings and a large population. There are also many special landmarks and social problems.

There are many kinds of buildings, some modern and some very old. For example, Centrepoint Tower, Queen Victoria Building, the Opera House and Hyde Park Barracks.

In most cities the population is made up of people from many different cultures. For instance, the population of Sydney is about 3.5 million. This includes people from Vietnam, Greece, Lebanon, Japan, Samoa and Yugoslavia.

Living in cities can create many problems because there are thousands of people living together. Firstly, problems arise like unemployment, homelessness and drugs. In addition, many street gangs can be found in cities.

There are both man-made and natural landmarks in all cities. These are usually popular tourist attractions. For example, in Sydney, Taronga Park Zoo, Harbour Bridge and Darling Harbour are very popular. There are also some natural landmarks that are tourist attractions such as Bondi Beach, the Great Barrier Reef and Kakadu National Park.

George (Age 11)

i. What is the social purpose and text type of Text 6.14?

....

....

....

ii. Comment on the following aspects of text organisation:
Text and paragraph previews:

....

....

....

Patterns of theme choice:

....

....

....

iii. Circle any examples of nominalisation.

iv. Highlight any text connectives and identify what type they are.

v. List any words that are related by the following types of lexical cohesion:

Class/sub-class	
Whole/part	
Synonyms	
Antonyms	
Repetition	
Collocation	

Exercise 6.17

The following texts by younger writers show how they are beginning to use the grammatical resources of theme and cohesion. However, they also illustrate some of the difficulties often experienced by developing writers. Read the texts and answer the questions that follow.

Text 6.15

Brachiosaurus was a reptile. He had a long tail and a long neck. He walked on four legs. He was a herbivore and it ate plants. He lived in water. They laid more than one egg.

Huong (Age 6)

i. Even though this writer uses experiential themes (ie. noun groups and pronouns) to focus on the topic of the report, there are problems with reference. Highlight the referring words. What do you notice?

....

....

....

ii. Underline any compound or complex sentences. How are the clauses in these sentences joined?

....

....

....

Text 6.16

Brontosaurus was a reptile. Brontosaurus was 20 metres long. Brontosaurus walked on 4 legs. Brontosaurus was a herbivore. Brontosaurus lived on land.

Kalid (Age 6)

i. Highlight the themes in Text 6.16. How could the student use reference to avoid this repetition?

....

....

....

ii. Text 6.16 sounds like a 'list'. How might the student combine some of the information in this 'list' of simple sentences?

....

....

....

Text 6.17

On Friday our class walked to Blackstump Creek to study the water environment. Our group had to record the different types of plants. First we looked at the water plants. We waded into the water to see what plants were growing in the shallow parts. Then we recorded it on the sheet of paper. Then we looked at the plants growing on the banks and then we had to sketch some of them. Then it was time to go back to school. Then we recorded our information on the computer.

i. What is the purpose and text type of Text 6.17?

....

....

....

ii. Highlight the themes (experiential and textual). How do they relate to the text's purpose?

....

....

....

iii. In terms of cohesion, how could this writer use text connectives more effectively? What other theme choices could help the writer sequence events in time (apart from 'then')?

....

....

....

....

Exercise 6.18

Use the following table to record your understanding of the key terms introduced in this chapter.

Term	Your understanding of the term
Textual function of language	
Text preview	
Paragraph preview	
Theme	
Experiential theme	
Interpersonal theme	
Textual theme	
Text connective	
Conjunction	
Thematic patterns	
Active voice	
Passive voice	
Nominalisation	
Cohesion	
Reference	

(continued)

Ellipsis	
Substitution	
Lexical cohesion	
Text connectives	

7 Learning and language across primary school (and beyond)

In previous chapters we looked at the key grammatical resources used for learning at school. We explored how these resources are used in different text types and in different curriculum areas. In this chapter we will look at how language also varies according to the different domains[1] in which learning occurs and, to a large degree, according to the different stages of school learning.

7.1 The domains of learning and language

Domains can be understood as the different places, 'worlds' or broad contexts in which learning occurs. Three domains have been identified as particularly important for students as they move through the stages of schooling. These are:

- The everyday and familiar world of home and the community (**everyday** domain)

- The specialised subject areas within schooling (**specialised** domain)

- The often contradictory and socially diverse world within and beyond schooling (**critical** or reflexive domain).

The everyday domain of learning is associated with commonsense knowledge, which is generally passed on orally by participation in activities with parents or caregivers who are familiar to the child. While everyday learning continues to be relevant at school (eg. observing and sharing understandings as a starting point for many topics), this learning is mainly associated with the home and community. The language associated with everyday learning is generally spoken, informal and concerned with topics of immediate experience.

The specialised domain of learning refers to the systematised learning that occurs in mainstream educational institutions. This learning is based on classification systems and understandings that are different from those we operate with in everyday life. For example, ways of classifying or grouping food items in the everyday domain may be according to where they are bought or kept or which meals they are related to. In the specialised domain, however, these items would be more likely classified according to scientific categories (eg. carbohydrates, proteins, vitamins). The language associated with the specialised domain is increasingly discipline specific, technical, formal, generalised and involving a range of modes, especially the organised written and diagrammatic modes.

---

[1] The concept of domains was developed by Mary Macken-Horarik (1996) in the context of research within junior secondary schooling. However, domains are understood as important across all areas of learning.

The critical domain (which is also termed the **reflexive** domain) is where the knowledge built up in specialised and everyday domains is questioned and problematised. Language is used in the critical domain to deal with complex and often contradictory issues. Not only will it be constructed through a variety of media, but will allow for negotiation with people who may have different perspectives.

Language development across the domains of learning

While in general we can locate most of the learning which occurs in primary (and secondary) schooling within the specialised domain of learning, learning can be seen as a development across these domains. According to Mary Macken-Horarik (1996):

> ... learning in any domain is a product of the relationship with the one adjacent to it. Students build up the meaning potential of specialized contexts—its registers—on the basis of the prior learning they have done in the everyday world. And they begin to move into reflexive learning by challenging the understandings they have established in the specialized domain. (244)

In general, we expect students beginning schooling to be using language associated with the everyday domain. However, as they move through primary school they need to use language associated with the specialised domain of learning. Students also need to be prepared for the critical domain in order to participate fully in learning within and beyond primary school. The development of learning and language occurs through active participation with support from others (eg. teachers). It also occurs across the domains in a number of different dimensions, which are outlined in Figure 7.1.

Figure 7.1: Development of learning and language across the domains

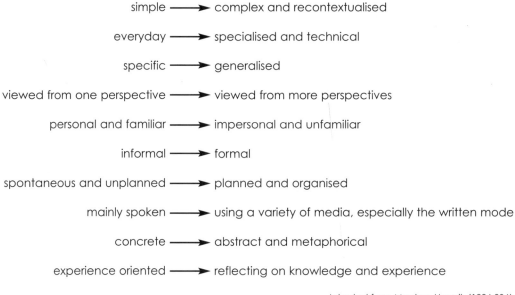

Adapted from Macken-Horarik (1996:236)

The development of language and learning shown in Figure 7.1 can be seen across the stages of the curriculum and across specific units of work or topics.

Development across the stages of the curriculum

Language and learning develop across the stages of primary school (and beyond). This is reflected in outcome statements in every curriculum area. Look, for example, at the following examples of specific outcomes (indicators) from Early Stage 1 and Stage 3 in the NSW Human Society and Its Environment syllabus. Note how they reflect the development across some of the dimensions outlined in Figure 7.1.

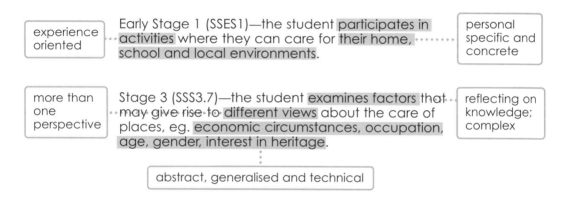

Development across units of work

Similar development can also be seen in programming for a unit of work. For example, units of work generally begin with building shared understandings which are familiar and concrete before moving to less familiar, more specialised and often problematic areas of the topic. The following outline of the English unit we examined in Chapter 2 illustrates a shift from the language uses associated with the everyday domain to those needed to participate in specialised and critical domains of learning.

Table 7.1: Development across a unit of work

Sequence of teaching and learning activities	Predicted uses of language
Send introductory email to other participants in Bookrap	Everyday, personal (about self), informal; using a variety of media
Reading a range of picture books shortlisted for Children's Book Council of Australia awards	Everyday but beyond 'own world'; informal
Read background information on authors	Impersonal and unknown
Give personal opinions on favourite book and justify opinions	Viewed from one perspective but reflecting on knowledge and experiences
Respond to opinions of other rappers	More complex and recontextualised
Explain how the techniques used by the illustrator and writer work together to create meaning	Technical; generalised; planned and organised
Critically assess one of the shortlisted books	Viewed from a variety of perspectives

Adapted from *Bookweek-Picture Books* rap 2001,
Professional Support and Curriculum NSW Department of Education and Training

As we can see in Table 7.1, the development from everyday to more specialised and critical uses of language does not always occur evenly. For example, some children may be confidently using a variety of media while still dealing with concrete and everyday topics. Similarly, some children at an early stage of learning are able to build quite technical classification systems of phenomena which interest them (eg. types of dinosaurs) and to use associated technical terminology.

7.2 Text types across the domains and stages of learning

The development of learning and language outlined above can be seen in the different text types which are used in different domains and at different stages of schooling. Research into language and learning has found that the text types students need for learning become more complex as children move through schooling[2]. In fact many of the elemental text types found in primary syllabus documents can be seen as belonging to groups or families of text types which are closely related in purpose and structure but which are more or less complex. Families of text types which are important to learning across the domains and stages of learning include:

- Recount text types—including personal recount and factual recount. Factual recount can be further classified as autobiographical, biographical and historical recounts.

[2] Much of this research was conducted by the NSW Department of Education and Training Disadvantaged Schools Program Metropolitan East Region) within the *Write it Right* project (Coffin 1996; Humphrey 1996; Rothery 1994) .

- Explanation text types—including sequential explanations (concerned with how processes occur) and causal explanations (concerned with why things occur).

- Response text types—including personal response, review and critical response (challenging the message or commonly held interpretations of a text).

- Argument text types—including exposition, analytical exposition (which includes evidence from authoritative sources) and challenge (arguing against commonly held interpretations).

Table 7.2 illustrates how text types from these families as well as others which are important in primary schooling are used in different domains of learning.

Table 7.2: Text types in different domains

Domains of learning		
Everyday	Specialised	Critical
Observation *(eg. What did we see at the zoo?)* Comment *(eg. Did you enjoy the trip to the zoo?)* Anecdote Personal recount Personal response *(eg. What did you like most about the book?)* Instructions *(eg. Now take out your pencils please children)*	Literary description Factual description Information report Factual recount (autobiographical, biographical and historical) Literary recount Narrative Review Procedure Explanation (sequential and causal) Exposition	Analytical Exposition *(including evidence to refute opposing arguments)* Discussion Challenge *(eg. Critically assess Australia's policy on refugees)* Critical response *(eg. How do advertisements reinforce stereotypes about the aged?)* Evaluation *(eg. evaluation of an experimental design)*

Adapted from Macken-Horarik (1996:246)

Most text types included in primary school syllabus documents are located within the specialised domain. In fact, we can say that these text types are **privileged** in the primary school curriculum. This means that these text types are more often used by teachers and that students are more often rewarded in assessment tasks for producing them. However, the text types of the everyday domain provide an essential starting point for those needed in the specialised (primary school) domain. Text types from the critical domain are normally found in the secondary and tertiary contexts. To effectively create texts in the critical domain students need to have good control over the specialised text types.

Here are three examples within the response family which represent choices which are privileged in different domains.

Text 7.1: Personal Response

The Deltora Quest

I liked The Deltora Quest because it was a really exciting story. I liked Jasmine and Lief best but I also liked the little Kin because he was really cute.

Text 7.1 provides positive observations about the story and particular characters. Like most personal response text types, evaluations are made according to how the writer is emotionally affected. The comments seem to be presented in the order in which they occur to the writer with no obvious planning.

Text 7.2: Review

Fox

Fox is an interesting picture book written by Margaret Wild and illustrated by Ron Brooks. It is a story of a friendship between a magpie and a dog, which is challenged by an evil Fox.

The illustrations in the book are very effective because they seem quick and rough but they are really sophisticated and full of texture. Oil and chalk and charcoal are used effectively to give a bushy feeling.

The writing seems messy like a draft but this mulches with the outback pictures. The writing and pictures work together for the exact effect that the writer and illustrator wanted.

Fox is a beautiful and meaningful story, suitable for all ages.

Text 7.2 also provides evaluations of a story, however, these include understandings of how the text was constructed and of the message of the text. The writer shows a technical knowledge of writing and illustration and is able to generalise about how the techniques are used to create particular effects on the reader. The text is planned and organised according to different aspects of the text construction (eg. writing, illustration).

Text 7.3: Critical Response

Harry Potter and the Order of the Phoenix

Harry Potter and the Order of the Phoenix is the fifth book in the Harry Potter series. In this book J.K. Rowling has attempted to show the wizarding world as more complex than in the other books. Harry and the other 'heroes' like James, his father, are shown us not always so heroic. We see Harry as moody and unreasonably angry at times and James as often quite a nasty young man. The author also makes us feel some sympathy for Snape, as we see how badly he was treated by James as a boy.

However, despite these attempts, the world presented in the Harry Potter series is still oversimplified and the characters are stereotypical. It is only wizard characters who are presented as complex. Muggles, represented by Harry's aunt, uncle and cousin are still presented as stupid and afraid with no hope of change and goblins are always *obsessed with money. Even sympathetic characters like Hermione and Ron and Professor McGonagall seem to be caricatures rather than personalities.*

There is no doubt that J.K. Rowling knows how to tell a good story. However many of the characters in these stories are stereotypical and are not presented as real personalities.

In this text, the writer has included positive evaluations of the 'crafting' of the book, however, the effectiveness of this crafting is also challenged. As with Text 7.2, the writer is able to generalise by grouping the characters. Although these characters are evaluated (eg. *stupid, afraid, nasty, angry*), the focus is on evaluating how realistic the crafting of these characters has been (eg. *complex, stereotypical, the author makes us feel sympathy*). The text is structured in such a way that the more expected or mainstream perspective on the characters is included but is then problematised so that the reader is led towards accepting the writer's interpretation as the final word.

Developing complexity within families of text type

Development of complexity within text types and text type families can be achieved in a number of ways. Some of these include:

- Incorporating elemental text types (or stages from these) within other text types (eg. explanations providing evidence for exposition and discussion text types; literary or factual description within narrative text types; narrative and recount within reviews).

- Adding text types which are the same or different to create Macro text types in the form of projects.

- Including evidence from named and/or referenced sources to support and refute arguments and perspectives within expositions, discussions, and reviews.

- Including arguments from other perspectives within exposition and review text types. These arguments are often included as a 'concession' within an argument so that it can be refuted immediately (eg. *Although logging creates employment, it greatly damages the environment.*)

- Incorporating multiple complications and partial resolutions within a narrative to heighten the suspense.

- Building multiple 'worlds' within fantasy, historical or science fiction narratives. This involves describing a number of scenes (which often draw on specialised or technical knowledge) and developing sequences of events in the 'real' world as well as in the imagined or 'other' world.

- Including a range of modes in presenting texts (eg. verbal and visual elements working together to create meaning; 'dynamic text' available through computer technology).

Text 7.4 and 7.5 are examples of complex text types which illustrate some of these features.

Text 7.4: Exposition (Analytical)

Do you think rainforest logging should be stopped in Australia?		
Thesis	At present much of the rainforest area of Australia is logged by selective or clearfelling methods. *While the logging industry argues that logging should be continued because of the employment it creates and the need for rainforest timber,* there is strong evidence that logging practices cause significant damage to the environment and therefore should be phased out.	*Concession to 2nd perspective*
Argument 1	The most important reason for phasing out logging is its impact on the environment. Firstly, rainforests provide a habitat for many species of rare and/or endangered animals which have evolved to suit the conditions there. If the rainforests are logged, many of these species will become extinct. *Although supporters of logging argue that rainforests regenerate quickly,* biological scientists have found that new forests do not provide the same variety of vegetation and young trees do not have hollows which act as habitats for many animals.	*Concession to 2nd perspective* Evidence from outside 'authority'
Argument 2	Rainforest soils are also affected by removing trees. When the canopy of trees is removed by logging, large areas of soils are left exposed to rain and wind. The water and nutrients are transported out of the area by the rain and the wind resulting in soil erosion.	Explanation sequence as evidence
Argument 3	Finally there are political reasons for ceasing logging. *Although supporters of logging claim that conservationists represent only a small proportion of the population,* a recent opinion poll commissioned by the National Conservation Foundation found that 69 per cent of people in New South Wales favour preserving rainforests. This shows that rainforest protection is an important conservation issue.	*Concession to 2nd perspective* Evidence from outside 'authority'
Reinforcement of thesis	The arguments presented above make it clear that continuing to log rainforests would be irresponsible. Therefore logging should be phased out over the next few years and other industries such as eco-tourism should be encouraged in rainforests.	

Text 7.5: Historical Narrative

The First Prime Minister		
Orientation	"Come on, Ed! Time for bed! You can finish your project in the morning." Ed reluctantly pushed his history books aside.	
	"I wonder what it would be like to be a Prime Minister?" he pondered as he slowly prepared for bed. *A little later, as Ed lay in bed, his thoughts took him back to the time of Federation.*	*Bridge to 'other world'*
Autobiographical Recount (extra stage integrated in Narrative)	He was Edmund Barton, on his way to Centennial Park for the Federation ceremonies. He would be officially sworn in as the first Prime Minister of Australia. As the horse and carriage proceeded along Grand Drive, Edmund wondered about the decisions he had already made with his cabinet ministers. He had promised to give women the vote. And he had decided to send troops to the Boer War. He squirmed in his seat. Was it really right for Australia to be fighting a war for Britain so far away?	*Imaginary recreation of historical events* Critical reflection on events
Complication	Suddenly Ed's thoughts were interrupted by a loud shot. The horses reared and bolted out of control through the screaming crowd. Edward shouted loudly at the guards "Help, get me out of here!"	
Resolution	*"Eddie, Eddie, wake up. You've been dreaming!"* "What? Where am I?" Edward sat up to find his mother leaning over the bed holding him tightly.	*Return to 'original world'*
Coda	"Oh Mum, I don't think I'm ready to be Prime Minister just yet."	

Both Texts 7.4 and 7.5 need to be seen as products of learning across domains. In Text 7.4 we see evidence that the student has been able to successfully reproduce knowledge valued within the mainstream Science and HSIE curriculum areas and to use conventions of the written mode to organise that knowledge as evidence for an exposition text type. Evidence of a critical perspective to that knowledge is shown by how the student draws on specialised knowledge to consider an issue which is relevant, not only to the immediate school curriculum but to the wider social and political context.

In Text 7.5 the student shows evidence of the learning they have done in everyday domains where passing on cultural values through stories is a widely practiced activity. The student also shows evidence of sophisticated specialised knowledge across the curriculum—drawing both on historically accurate events and on knowledge of narrative structure. In building multiple worlds and incorporating historical events as an additional stage, the student shows that they are able to manipulate the knowledge of elemental narrative structure.

7.3 Development of grammatical resources across domains

In Chapters 4, 5 and 6 we explored the grammatical resources associated with the three functions of language—experiential, interpersonal and textual. As children develop understandings of language associated with everyday, specialised and critical domains of learning, they will need knowledge of an increasingly broad range of resources from the three areas of meaning. In this section we will describe some important grammatical resources associated with children's learning across the primary school years and beyond.

As with text types, it is possible to see the development of grammatical resources on a continuum. However, the critical and specialised domains of learning generally draw on similar resources.

Experiential meanings—language for representing experience

Children need knowledge of a variety of lexical and grammatical resources for naming and describing phenomena as they move from everyday domains to specialised and critical domains of learning. Table 7.3 shows the development of some of the language for representing experience across these domains.

Table 7.3: Resources for representing experience

Everyday domains of learning ➝ Specialised and critical domains of learning	
Everyday vocabulary	Subject-specific and technical vocabulary (eg. *latitude, hexagonal, environment, narrative*) Formal (academic) vocabulary related to all subject areas (eg. *evidence, significant, resources*)
Particular nouns (eg. We saw a *shark* at the beach.)	Generalised nouns (eg. *Sharks* are fierce predators.)
Simple noun groups (eg. *A shark is a fish.*) Noun groups with simple descriptive adjectivals (eg. *big* teeth, *sharp* teeth)	Expanded noun groups, including: • Technical and classifying adjectivals in factual texts to give fine distinctions (eg. A shark is a *cartilaginous* fish.) • More sophisticated descriptive adjectivals to build images in literary texts (eg. The *monstrous* shark sped towards its *unlucky* victim.) • Adjectival clauses and phrases to add details to phenomena (eg. Sharks can detect small amounts *of electricity generated by their prey.*)
Everyday action verbs including phrasal verbs (eg. *burned down; eaten up*) Simple relating verbs for naming and describing phenomena (eg. *there is; it is; it has*)	Wide range of verbs including subject specific and formal action verbs (eg. *evaporate, migrate, demonstrate*) Wide range of relating verbs to identify, define, classify, describe phenomena (eg. *concern, relate to, mean, equal, occupy, represent, possess*)
Small range of simple adverbials mainly used for locating events in place and time (eg. *On the weekend; at bed time; in the morning; at home; at school; at the shops*)	Range of adverbial phrases and clauses to describe the circumstances of events in precise and detailed ways. These often include: • Details and images to develop chararacters, events and settings in literary texts (eg. she danced as *gracefully as a swan;* The lizard flicked his tongue *lazily, as it surveyed its victim.*) • Dates for accuracy in factual texts (eg. Toogong church was built *in 1872.*) • Precise locations and measurements (eg. Toogong is *on the Boree Creek, 320 kilometres west of Sydney.*) • Causes of phenomena (eg. The canola crop was small *because of the drought.*)

Texts 7.6, 7.7 and 7.8 are extracts from longer texts and have been annotated to show the grammatical resources used to express experiential meanings in the everyday domain and in the specialised and critical domains.

Text 7.6: Annotated example of text with *everyday experiential meanings*

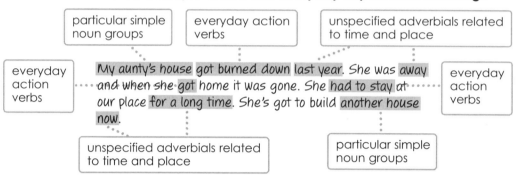

Text 7.7: Annotated example of factual text with *specialised experiential meanings*

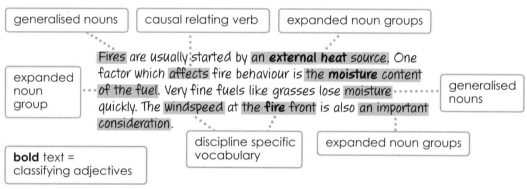

Text 7.8: Annotated example of literary text with *specialised experiential meanings*

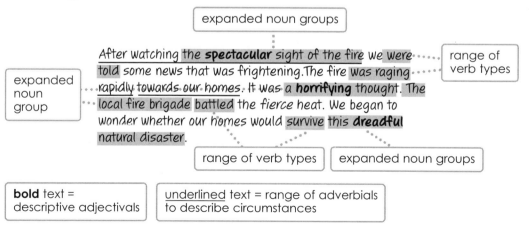

Table 7.4: Resources for interacting with others

Everyday domains of learning ➞	Specialised and critical domains of learning
Interruptions and overlapping turn taking in spoken interaction	Careful turn taking in spoken interaction
Use of Ist person pronouns as participants in action and sensing verbs to indicate personal perspective (eg. *I* think; *I* went; *I* like)	Little use of personal pronouns. Generalised, authoritative named and unnamed sources for opinions (eg. *experts agree; evidence suggests; Dr Martin says*) Concessive clauses and phrases to incorporate other perspectives (eg. *Although there is some debate about the issue* ...)
Imperative clauses used for commands (eg. *Give me a hand.*)	Interrogatives with modal verbs often used for commands (eg. *Would you mind giving me a hand?*)
Colloquial lexis, contractions, abbreviations and slang	Formal language, full forms of words
Vocatives such as first names, diminutives and nick-names	Titles or no names
Simple evaluative vocabulary with emotional value (Affect) Mainly: • mental verbs (eg. I *loved* the movie) • adjectivals (eg. the movie was *good*)	Institutionalised evaluative vocabulary that is to do with worth, effectiveness and qualities rather than personal judgements—(Judgement and Appreciation) (eg. It was a *well crafted* movie.) Range of evaluative vocabulary to build description and suspense in literary texts. These include: • Adjectivals, verbs, noun groups and adverbials • Indirect expressions of Affect (eg. She blushed at the thought.) • Metaphors and similes (eg. Butterflies leapt in her stomach; He danced like a butterfly.)
Simple grading expressions used to amplify meanings or 'turn up volume' (eg. it was *really* big)	More formal grading expressions used to qualify assertions in factual texts (eg. A *significant* proportion) Range of grading expressions to vary the intensity of events and descriptions in literary texts, including: • adverbial and adjectival graders (eg. The *ear piercing* scream; He screamed *loudly*) • Graded 'core' meanings of words (eg. She *pelted* to the door; he *hurried* to the door) • Repetition (eg. I *slowly, slowly* crept along)
Straightforward expressions of modality—modal verbs or adverbs (eg. Emus *can't* fly.)	Less straightforward ways of expressing modality— interpersonal metaphors (eg. *It is possible that* ...)

Interpersonal meanings—language for interacting with others

The resources needed for interacting with others also vary in the move from everyday to specialised and critical uses of language. Interacting in the everyday domain is marked by more personal, familiar and informal language, while interaction in the specialised and critical domains is marked by more impersonal and formal uses of language. Lexical and grammatical resources for expressing interactions in these domains are shown in Table 7.4.

Texts 7.9, 7.10 and 7.11 are extracts of texts which have been annotated to show the grammatical resources used to express interpersonal meanings in the everyday domain and in the specialised and critical domains.

Text 7.9: Annotated example of dialogue with *everyday interpersonal meanings*

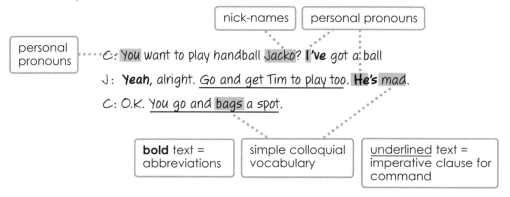

Text 7.10: Annotated example of one argument of a factual exposition with *specialised* and *critical interpersonal meanings*

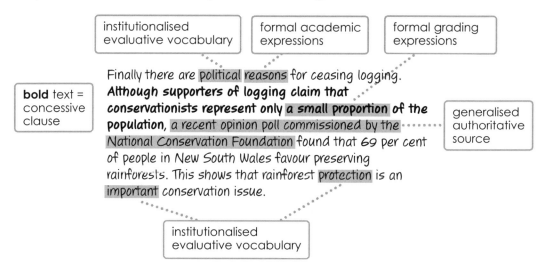

Text 7.11: Annotated example of a literary text with *specialised* and *critical* interpersonal meanings

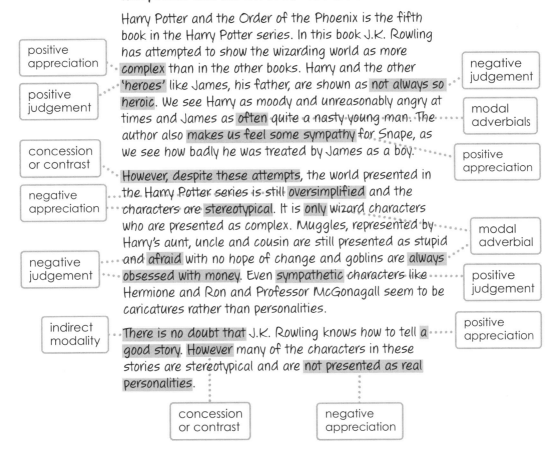

Harry Potter and the Order of the Phoenix

Harry Potter and the Order of the Phoenix is the fifth book in the Harry Potter series. In this book J.K. Rowling has attempted to show the wizarding world as more complex than in the other books. Harry and the other 'heroes' like James, his father, are shown as not always so heroic. We see Harry as moody and unreasonably angry at times and James as often quite a nasty young man. The author also makes us feel some sympathy for Snape, as we see how badly he was treated by James as a boy.

However, despite these attempts, the world presented in the Harry Potter series is still oversimplified and the characters are stereotypical. It is only wizard characters who are presented as complex. Muggles, represented by Harry's aunt, uncle and cousin are still presented as stupid and afraid with no hope of change and goblins are always obsessed with money. Even sympathetic characters like Hermione and Ron and Professor McGonagall seem to be caricatures rather than personalities.

There is no doubt that J.K. Rowling knows how to tell a good story. However many of the characters in these stories are stereotypical and are not presented as real personalities.

Annotation labels: positive appreciation, positive judgement, concession or contrast, negative appreciation, negative judgement, indirect modality, negative judgement, modal adverbials, positive appreciation, modal adverbial, positive judgement, positive appreciation, concession or contrast, negative appreciation

Textual meanings—language for creating well organised and cohesive texts

The language needed to organise the information in a text and for creating cohesion across a text becomes increasingly important as students move into specialised and critical domains of learning. Table 7.5 shows some of the textual resources that are associated with the different domains.

Table 7.5: Resources for creating well organised and cohesive texts

Everyday domains of learning ➤	Specialised and critical domains of learning
Texts are spontaneous and unplanned.	Texts are planned and organised for different purposes. For example: • Around particular topics or aspects of the topic in Report text types • According to arguments in exposition and discussion text types • According to time in recount and narrative text types.
Texts are usually short spoken dialogues with no need for text and paragraph previews.	Longer monologic texts. Often need text and paragraph previews to organise information.
Themes often varied with little patterning.	A variety of theme patterns across texts according to purpose. For example: • Repeated use of experiential themes in report and description text types • Zig-Zag pattern in explanation and exposition text types • Themes used to foreground time, place, manner and interpersonal meanings in narrative text types.
Logical relations expressed as simple conjunctions functioning as textual themes to join clauses. (eg. but, and, then, so)	Logical relations expressed as: • Textual themes (text connectives) joining sentences and paragraphs (eg. Moreover, Therefore, Meanwhile) • Dependent clauses (often in theme position) (eg. *If logging is stopped*, many workers will lose their jobs) • Verbs and Adverbials within clauses (eg. That will *lead* to social upheaval; Rainforests are at risk *because of logging*)
Texts organised around concrete things and people, achieved by: • Simple noun groups with concrete nouns (eg. The trees) • Clauses with action verbs (eg. The people chop down trees)	Factual texts organised around abstract things and processes and the relationships between them. This is achieved by: • Simple sentences with relating verbs (eg. Continued logging of rainforests *causes* environmental problems) • Nominalisation used to package information into complex noun groups (eg. *Continued **logging** of rainforests* results in *environmental **damage***)
Reference points to objects and behaviours in the shared physical context—ie. outside the text. (eg. Look at *that over there!*)	Reference points back or forward to: • Words in the text itself • Sections of the co-text • Diagrams, tables and graphs accompanying text in factual texts.
Lexical cohesion mostly achieved by repetition and collocation.	Lexical cohesion achieved by a range of resources, including repetition, synonyms, antonyms, collocation, class/sub-class relations and part/whole relations

Texts 7.12, 7.13 and 7.14 are examples of texts which have been annotated to show the grammatical resources used to express textual meanings in the everyday domain and in the specialised and critical domains.

Text 7.12: Annotated example of *everyday textual meanings*

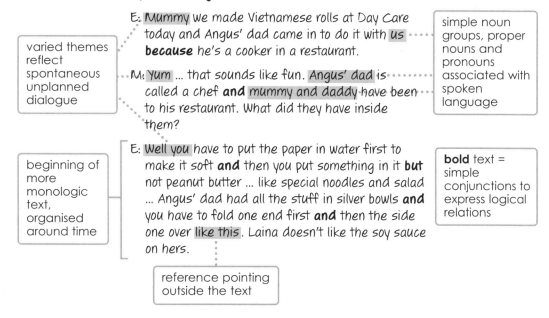

Spoken dialogue

varied themes reflect spontaneous unplanned dialogue

E: Mummy we made Vietnamese rolls at Day Care today and Angus' dad came in to do it with us **because** he's a cooker in a restaurant.

simple noun groups, proper nouns and pronouns associated with spoken language

M: Yum ... that sounds like fun. Angus' dad is called a chef **and** mummy and daddy have been to his restaurant. What did they have inside them?

beginning of more monologic text, organised around time

E: Well you have to put the paper in water first to make it soft **and** then you put something in it **but** not peanut butter ... like special noodles and salad ... Angus' dad had all the stuff in silver bowls **and** you have to fold one end first **and** then the side one over like this. Laina doesn't like the soy sauce on hers.

bold text = simple conjunctions to express logical relations

reference pointing outside the text

Text 7.13: Annotated extract of factual text showing *specialised* and *critical* textual meanings

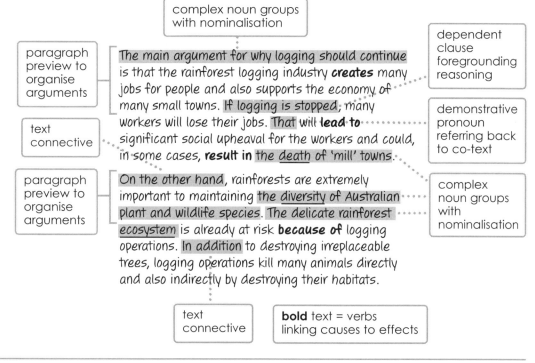

complex noun groups with nominalisation

paragraph preview to organise arguments

The main argument for why logging should continue is that the rainforest logging industry **creates** many jobs for people and also supports the economy of many small towns. If logging is stopped, many workers will lose their jobs. That will **lead to** significant social upheaval for the workers and could, in some cases, **result in** the death of 'mill' towns.

dependent clause foregrounding reasoning

text connective

demonstrative pronoun referring back to co-text

paragraph preview to organise arguments

On the other hand, rainforests are extremely important to maintaining the diversity of Australian plant and wildlife species. The delicate rainforest ecosystem is already at risk **because of** logging operations. In addition to destroying irreplaceable trees, logging operations kill many animals directly and also indirectly by destroying their habitats.

complex noun groups with nominalisation

text connective

bold text = verbs linking causes to effects

Text 7.14: Annotated example of literary text showing *specialised* and *critical* textual meanings.

The Dark Gloomy Night

noun group as theme setting scene

two circumstances used to signal beginning of complication stage

bold text = repetition of personal pronoun in theme position to track central participants

One dark gloomy night Jack and I were driving to the show. As we looked out the window, we saw lightning in the distance. **We** knew a storm was coming. The wind grew stronger and stronger and suddenly, without any warning, a huge gum tree fell behind us. Almost immediately, we heard an ear-splitting explosion as another bolt of lightening hit the tree in front of us. Feeling terrified, we carefully picked our way through the shattered branches. **We** drove along and realised that the storm had passed and now there was nothing but an eerie silence. "What on earth is that?!" whispered Jack. **We** stared at the tall, mysterious figure standing in the middle of the road. I gulped. This was all we needed.

dependent clause as theme foregrounding time

adverbial as theme foregrounding time

dependent clause as theme foregrounding interpersonal meaning through sensing verb (feeling)

adverbial as theme foregrounding time

Conclusion

In this chapter we have demonstrated a useful and flexible way of exploring the development of language across the primary years of schooling and beyond. In order to successfully participate in all curriculum areas of schooling, students need to move beyond the language of the everyday domain to the language of the specialised and critical domains of learning. This development occurs across the stages of primary and secondary schooling. It is possible to describe particular features of language associated with different domains, particularly with the move from the everyday to specialised domain. Knowledge of these features will assist teachers in planning for language development at each stage of learning. It is important to note here, however, that the development in students' language repertoires that we are referring to in this chapter does not take place 'naturally'. Rather it occurs in social contexts (usually those of schooling and other educational institutions) in interaction with language-aware teachers.[2]

---

[2] These understandings of teaching and learning, associated with the concept of **scaffolding** are based on the theoretical work of Lev Vygotsky (1962) and of Jerome Bruner (1978). We recommend that teachers who would like to explore the processes of teaching and learning language in more depth refer also to Gibbons (2002) and Hammond (2001).

Appendix

This Appendix contains descriptions and examples of the factual and literary text types introduced in Chapter 2 (Table 2.2). The example texts have been written by students with varying degrees of control over the structure and grammatical features associated with each text type.

Further examples of the different text types along with teaching notes for working with grammar and texts across the different stages of schooling can be found in the *English K-6 Modules* (NSW Board of Studies: 1998) downloadable as a PDF file from the NSW Board of Studies website.
<http://www.bosnsw-k6.nsw.edu.au>

Factual description

Social purpose

Factual descriptions describe the characteristic features of particular people, places or objects. These texts are not always a 'distinct' text type and are often embedded in other longer text types.

Structure

- Identification—an optional stage which gives a general orientation to the topic; used only when the description is a 'stand alone' text
- Description—a simple description of features or characteristics of the topic.

Key grammatical features

- Use of particular nouns
- Use of detailed noun groups to describe features or characteristics
- Use of different types of adjectives and adjectival phrases and clauses to form complex noun groups
- Use of relating verbs to define, describe and classify
- Use of action verbs to describe activities and behaviours
- Use of adverbials to provide extra detail about *where, how, with what* etc.
- Lexical cohesion achieved largely by repetition, class/sub-class and whole/part relationships.

Text A.1: Factual description

The Dentist

Identification A dentist is a special kind of doctor who helps clean your teeth and lets you know if there is something wrong with them.

Description He pulls out your teeth if they are too sick. Sometimes you can just go to the dentist to check your teeth but sometimes you go for fillings. A dentist works in a dentist surgery. A dentist uses a drill and toothbrush, mirror, a bib, lamp, tap, sucker, pick and water.

Information report

Social purpose

Information reports are used to give generalised information about an entire class of things, eg. snakes, cities, computers, rocks etc.

Structure

- General statement—identifies the subject of the report; may define or classify it
- Description—expanded descriptions of various 'aspects' such as parts, attributes, types, uses, behaviours, appearance, location, etc.

Key grammatical features

- Use of general nouns; may include technical nouns
- Use of quantity, factual and classifying adjectives to build descriptions in expanded noun groups
- Use of adjectival phrases and clauses to add detail to noun groups
- Repeated naming of the topic as theme
- Use of relating verbs to describe and classify the topic; action verbs to describe activities and behaviours
- Use of adverbials of place and manner
- Use of simple present tense to indicate the 'general' nature of the information
- Use of compound and complex sentences to give information. However, a combination of expanded noun groups and relating verbs often result in simple sentences in well developed information reports
- Lexical cohesion showing class/sub-class, whole/part relationships between words.

Text A.2: Information report

Triangles

General statement	A triangle is a geometric shape with three sides and three angles.
Description	An isosceles triangle has two sides and angles that that are the same and one that is different. A right angled triangle has a 90° angle.
	A scalene triangle has no sides or angles the same.
	In an equilateral triangle all the sides and angles are the same.

Text A.3: Information report

Toogong (spoken report)

General statement	Today I am going to speak about a small rural community called Toogong where my grandparents live.
Description (town name)	Toogong is an Aboriginal name which is said to mean 'a smoky fire near water' in the Wiradjuri language. It was probably a favourite hunting and camping place for Aboriginal people before European people came to Australia.
Description (location)	Toogong is located over the Blue Mountains about 320 kilometres west of Sydney. The Boree Creek runs through Toogong on its way to the Lachlan River. Mount Canobolas stands out as a landmark. It is an extinct volcano and the highest mountain west of the Blue Mountains. When it was active the volcanic lava flowed down the Boree Creek and that is why the land is so fertile near Toogong.
Description (primary products)	The main products from the farms around Toogong are wheat, oats and canola. Sheep and cattle are also fattened to sell for meat. More recently, grapes and olives are also important enterprises.

Jenny (Age 7)

Procedure

Social purpose

Procedures tell how to make or do something by giving a sequence of steps to follow (eg. instructions, directions, rules and recipes).

Structure

- The goal of the activity—an indication of what you are trying to do or make
- Materials—a list of materials (or ingredients/equipment etc.) needed to achieve the goal
- Steps—the sequence of steps that need to be followed.

Note: These stages are often signalled by headings in the text.

Key grammatical features

- Use of action verbs as commands
- Use of action verbs specific to the field (ie. art, cooking, science and technology etc.)
- Use of text connectives to indicate the sequence of steps (if not numbered)
- Use of adverbials and dependent clauses to express important details such as place, extent, manner
- Use of dependent clauses to express conditions, reasons, consequences, warnings etc. in more complex procedures
- Action verbs, adverbials (and in more complex procedures, dependent clauses) as theme.

Text A.4: Procedure

Goal (Heading) | **Making the cover of my portfolio**

Materials needed

Materials
Large sheet of art paper

Blue edicol dye

Oil pastel crayons

Cardboard pieces

Yellow, green, orange and red acrylic paint

Steps

Steps
1. Paint a blue background on a large sheet of art paper, using blue edicol dye.

2. Fold art paper in half.

3. Draw three waratahs using red oil pastel crayons on the right side of the art paper.

4. Dip different lengthed cardboard strips into paint to make the line patterns of the Banksia, the Bottlebrush, leaves and stems.

6. Dip the tip of your little finger into the yellow paint and print the Wattle.

7. Paste wood glue all over your artwork to make it shiny.

Rosemary (Age 8)

Procedural recount

Social purpose

To record the steps taken to carry out an investigation. Particularly important for recording practical learning experiences in Science and Technology such as experiments and data collection.

Structure

- Aim—provides a context by stating the purpose of the investigation; may also locate the investigation in time and place
- Record of events—sequential record of the methods or activities used in the investigation
- Results—what happened; a statement of the results, findings etc.

Key grammatical features

- Use of particular nouns (or pronouns) to name people, places and things
- Use of action verbs (past tense) to refer to the activities in the Events stage; sensing verbs (eg. we saw) in the results stage; relating verbs to introduce any technical concepts (eg. means, is called)
- References to 'time' in theme position—expressed by time connectives, time adverbials or dependent clauses
- Expressions of cause and effect (verbs, connectives, dependent clauses) and relating verbs may be used in Results stage
- Lexical cohesion showing use of repetition, synonym, class/sub-class and part/whole relationships.

Text A.5: Procedural recount

The water cycle

Aim

Today we did an experiment to demonstrate the energy of the sun and to construct a model of the water cycle.

Record of events

First we filled a third of a bucket with water that contained a cup of soil, a handful of salt and several leaves. We then put a mound of plasticine in the bottom of the bucket and stuck a plastic cup onto the mound with Blutack. Next we placed Clingwrap over the bucket and taped it down to make it secure. We put three of four marbles directly over the cup so that the plastic sagged and left it in the sun for a few hours.

Results

When we came back we saw that the water evaporated to the clingwrap where it cooled and condensed. Then the droplets joined together and then it fell into the cup. This is called precipitation. The water was clean because the sun only pulls up water not salt. This means that we had made a model of the water cycle.

Year 4 Joint Construction

Factual recount

Social purpose

Factual recounts tell us 'what happened' by documenting a series of events and evaluating their significance. They might be historical recounts, autobiographical or biographical recounts. Factual recounts may also be used to record events and observations from field trips and excursions.

Structure

- Orientation—sets a context for understanding the events that follow; provides background information about who, where, when, etc.
- Record of events—recounted in chronological order
- Reorientation—'rounds off' the sequence of events usually by resetting events in time.

Key grammatical features

- Use of particular nouns (or pronouns) to name people, places and things
- Use of general human and non-human nouns in historical recounts, where the focus is on generalising about events and the actions of groups of people
- Use of action verbs (past tense) to refer to the events
- References to 'time' in theme position—expressed by conjunctions, time connectives, time adverbials or dependent clauses
- Lexical cohesion showing use of repetition, synonyms and collocation
- Uses the resources of Judgement and Appreciation to evaluate behaviours and events.

	Text A.6: Factual recount
	Federation
Orientation	More than one hundred years after Captain James Cook and many other explorers landed on the soil of Australia, there was Federation.
Record of events	Before Federation people disagreed and agreed about becoming a nation. From 1850 to 1891, Sir Henry Parkes debated for federation in his newspaper, The Empire. In 1891 the first Australian convention happened and many people supported the idea, such as Edmund Barton. On the first of January, 1901, the British Government finally allowed all six states to join to become one nation.
Reorientation	Federation is a very important historical event for Australia because it meant that all the states were united.
	Kaiwen (Age 10)

Explanation

Social purpose

To explain scientifically how technological and natural phenomena come into being, ie. how or why things occur. Sequential explanations are concerned with the sequence or phases of a process—how a process occurs (eg. the life cycle of a butterfly). Causal explanations are concerned with causes of events—why a process occurs (eg. why tidal waves occur).

Structure

- Identification—identifies and gives general information about the phenomenon
- Explanation sequence—a temporal sequence of the main phases of a process or a cause and effect sequence of events.

Key grammatical features

- Use of general, abstract, technical, non-human nouns
- Factual and classifying adjectivals to describe phenomenon
- Action verbs in the simple present tense to express events; relating verbs to do with cause/effect
- Use of time conjunctions, time/sequencing connectives and time adverbials (as themes) to sequence events in sequential explanations
- Use of causal conjunctions, causal connectives and causal adverbials (as themes) in causal explanations
- Use of passive voice to foreground the object undergoing the process
- Use of nominalisation to summarise events and name abstract phenomena.

	Text A.7: Explanation (Sequential)
	Making paper from woodchips
Identification	Woodchipping is a process used to obtain pulp and paper products from forest trees.
Explanation sequence (temporal)	The woodchipping process begins when the trees are cut down in a selected area of forest called a coupe. After that the tops and branches are cut off. The logs are then dragged to a log landing where they are loaded onto a truck. Next the bark of the log is removed and then the logs are taken to chipper. The chipper cuts the logs into small pieces called woodchips. After this, the woodchips are screened to remove dirt and other impurities. At this stage, the woodchips are either exported or made into pulp. The pulp is then bleached and the water content removed. Finally it is rolled out to make paper.

Text A.8: Explanation (Causal)

How does a dynamo work?

Identification

A dynamo is a machine which changes mechanical energy into electrical energy. It is also called a generator.

Explanation sequence *(cause and effect)*

When the axle of a dynamo is turned, it receives mechanical energy. The mechanical energy of the axle is transferred to a coil which then spins between the two poles of a magnet. Because a magnetic force acts on electrons in the wire of the coil, they begin to move. The movement of electrons causes electrical energy. The electrical energy powers a light bulb which then lights up.

Exposition

Social purpose

Expositions are persuasive text types that argue a case for or against a particular point of view. Some expositions persuade the reader to think in a certain way by accepting a theory or position (eg. that smoking is bad for your health). Others persuade the reader to act in a certain way (eg. to build a playground in the local park).

Structure

- i. Background—provides a context for your argument by introducing the issue; particularly important in more developed expositions

  ii. Statement of position—what it is you are trying to convince the reader of (sometimes called a *thesis*); usually followed by a preview of the arguments being used to support this position

- Series of arguments—arguments are ordered logically (according to the text preview if there is one); well developed texts use paragraphs (with a paragraph preview and supporting evidence) for each new argument

- Reinforcement of position—re-affirms the writer's point of view in the light of the arguments presented.

Key grammatical features

- Use of nominalisation to name issues, arguments, reasons, etc.

- Some use of technical nouns in the evidence

- Thinking (sensing) verbs to express opinion in a straightforward, explicit way; interpersonal metaphor used to express opinion in a less straightforward, implicit way

- Varying degrees of modality to temper arguments and express opinion

- Use of textual themes (text connectives) to introduce and link arguments

- Use of evaluative vocabulary, especially Judgement and Appreciation; expressions of feeling using Affect are not valued in more developed expositions.

Text A.9: Exposition

Dogs

Statement of Position	I think dogs make good pets.
Argument 1	One reason dogs can make good pets is because they are very active and playful. They are cute and you can teach them tricks.
Argument 2	Another reason dogs make good pets is because you can take them for walks and they could protect you.
Reinforcement of Position	These are the main reasons why dogs make good pets but you have to look after them.

Discussion

Social purpose

Discussions are used to look at an issue from a range of perspectives, before making a judgement or recommendation.

Structure

- Identification—provides a context for the discussion by introducing the issue and giving any relevant background information; may preview in a general way, the different points of view
- Arguments for and against—paragraphs used to present arguments for both sides
- Conclusion/recommendation—sums up both sides and makes a recommendation favouring one side.

Key grammatical features

- Use of nominalisation to name issues, arguments, reasons, advantages, disadvantages, etc.
- Use of adjectivals to condense information into the noun groups
- Use of a wide variety of text connectives to introduce and link arguments logically
- Thinking (sensing) verbs to express opinion in a straightforward, explicit way; interpersonal metaphor used to express opinion in a less straightforward, implicit way
- Varying degrees of modality to temper arguments and express opinion
- Use of dependent (concessive) clauses to acknowledge and weaken evidence of opposing argument
- Use of Judgement vocabulary to evaluate the behaviour of individuals and groups
- Use of Appreciation vocabulary to assess significance and importance
- Use of synonyms, antonyms and repetition to emphasise arguments.

Text A.10: Discussion

School uniforms

Identification	The issue of whether or not we should wear school uniforms is very important for us to consider. There are good reasons both for and against this.
Arguments For	Firstly, we need to consider the reasons why we should wear school uniforms. One reason is that school uniforms make life easier. They are also usually easy to clean and they save a lot of time and arguments in the morning because children know what to wear and where to find it. Another reason is that if you wear school uniform people don't know whether you come from a wealthy or poor family which can prevent teasing and discrimination in schools. They can also take away peer group pressure which can prevent stress and unhappiness at school.
Arguments Against	There are also some reasons why children should not have to wear school uniforms. Firstly, wearing exactly the same thing as everybody else, day after day can be boring and uninspiring. Sometimes children like to express themselves by wearing different clothes. School uniforms don't stop peer pressure. Unfortunately it is there all the time and children need to learn how to deal with it. Secondly, children need to have experience making decisions which concern them. If they don't they will never learn to make decisions as adults. The third reason is that school is supposed to be for learning not about being all the same. Making a fuss about uniform just takes away attention from the important things about school.
Conclusion/ Recommendation	In summary, although there are many advantages of wearing school uniforms, in the end the disadvantages outweigh these advantages. Therefore I think children should not be forced to wear school uniform.

Literary description

Social purpose

Literary descriptions describe the characteristic features of a particular person, place or object (often imaginative). They are not always a 'distinct' text type and are often embedded in literary texts such as narratives.

Structure

- Identification—an optional stage which gives a general orientation to the subject; used only when the description is a 'stand alone' text
- Description—describes features or characteristics of the subject.

Key grammatical features

- Use of particular nouns
- Use of detailed noun groups to describe features or characteristics, incorporating a range of adjectivals to build descriptions
- Use of relating verbs to define and describe
- Use of action verbs to describe activities and behaviours
- Use of adverbials to provide extra detail about *where, how, with what* etc.
- Lexical cohesion achieved largely by synonyms, antonyms, collocation
- Use of Affect, Judgement and Appreciation vocabulary to evaluate phenomena
- Use of figurative language such as simile, metaphor, personification, alliteration, atypical word combinations, 'invented' words, etc.
- Use of grading vocabulary to intensify descriptions.

Text A.11: Example embedded in a narrative

Description (no Orientation) The beast stared down at me. It was a horrific sight. It had a huge bulbous body with bloated pustules dripping green slimy liquid onto the floor. It's eight oversized legs ended with enormous shapeless feet which gripped the ground with wart like suckers. On its head were two lidless bulging red eyes and a gruesome piggy nose covered with slimy grey snot. More crater shaped pustules covered the surface of its head and the slime from these dripped into its grotesque mouth. What nightmare had I stumbled into?!

Rosemary and Lily (Age 9)

Narrative

Social purpose

To entertain and instruct through dealing with unusual and unexpected development of events. Narratives often convey messages about how people are expected to behave when faced with particular kinds of events in our culture.

Structure

- Orientation—describes a setting in time and place; introduces the main characters or narrator; orients the reader to what is to follow
- Complication—a sequence of events that may begin in a usual fashion but then change to include events that are unusual or problematic for one or more of the characters; characters may express their reaction to or evaluation of these events
- Resolution—deals with the attempts to solve or overcome the problem
- Coda—optional stage giving an overall evaluation of the events; may state how the character/s have changed or what has been learned.

Note: It is important not to see the structure of a narrative as fixed. However, students need to become familiar with this 'prototypical' description before they can begin to explore how these stages can be manipulated for rhetorical effect and to position the reader in certain ways (eg. no orientation, a series of complications before any resolution, partial or unsatisfactory resolutions, shunting between events in the past and present etc.)

Key grammatical features

- Use of particular nouns to refer to the central characters, objects and places
- Use of detailed noun groups to describe features or characteristics, incorporating a range of adjectivals to build descriptions
- Use of action verbs (usually past tense) to indicate activities and behaviours; characters often use saying and thinking verbs (ie. direct or indirect speech/thought)
- Use of adverbials and dependent clauses to express important details such as time, place, extent, manner etc.
- Lexical cohesion achieved largely by synonyms, antonyms, collocation
- Use of Affect, Judgement and Appreciation vocabulary to evaluate phenomena
- Use of figurative language such as simile, metaphor, personification, alliteration, atypical word combinations, 'invented' words, etc.
- Use of grading vocabulary to intensify descriptions.

Text A.12: Narrative

Katie's Show and Tell

Orientation

One day Kate found a spider in her back yard and decided to take it in for Show and Tell. She loved spiders and knew which ones were dangerous.

Complication

When it was her turn to do show and tell, Kate got up excitedly and opened the box to show everybody the spider. Suddenly the spider jumped out the box onto the floor. Everybody in the class started to scream and run around the

Embedded Evaluation

room madly. Kate thought they were stupid. It was only a spider. She got down and frantically started to look for it but everybody was in the way.

"What if they trod on it?" she thought angrily.

Resolution

Finally the teacher got mad and yelled at the kids to stay still. Then Kate was able to find the poor thing under the teacher's desk. It was shivering with fright but still alive. Kate

Coda

decided not to bring anything interesting to school anymore.

Harriet (Age 8)

Literary recount

Social purpose

To retell a series of events for the purpose of entertaining. Literary recounts involve personal or imagined experience.

Structure

- Orientation—sets a context for understanding the events that follow; provides background information about who, where, when, etc.
- Record of events—recounted in chronological order
- Reorientation—'rounds off' the sequence of events usually by resetting events in time.

Key grammatical features

- Use of particular nouns to refer to people, places and things
- Use of a range of adjectivals to build descriptions
- Use of action verbs (usually past tense) to indicate activities and behaviours; use of sensing and thinking verbs to indicate thoughts, feelings and what was said
- Use of adverbials and dependent clauses (often as Theme) to set events in time and place
- Lexical cohesion achieved largely by repetition, synonyms, collocation
- Use of Affect, Judgement and Appreciation vocabulary to evaluate phenomena
- Use of figurative language such as simile, metaphor, personification, alliteration, atypical word combinations, 'invented' words, etc.
- Use of grading vocabulary to intensify descriptions.

Text A.13: Literary recount

Dear Aunty Sally,

Orientation

How are you? Thankyou for the birthday money. For my birthday I got to choose what I wanted to do.

Record of events

In the morning I opened my presents. I got a fishing rod. We went fishing in the lake even though it's dirty. Dad told me that dough with cotton on it was good for medium sized fish. He sure was right as we caught a big cat fish with streaks on it.

In the evening I chose to go for pizza at the Croc Hotel. When we got there it had a skeleton hanging off the roof with the cotton over it for the web. That was for Halloween. After we finished our pizza, we ran around the hotel and even splashed around a bit in the pool. You're not supposed to but nobody caught us.

Reorientation

We had a great night and we didn't get home until about 11 o'clock. I'm looking forward to coming down as the mozzies are as bad as. See you in a few weeks.

Love Alex

Response

Social purpose

Response text types are used to summarise, analyse and respond to literary texts, artworks or performances. They may take the form of a personal response or a review.

Structure

Personal response:

- Context—gives background information
- Opinion/reaction—looks at the qualities of the text, artwork or performance and expresses personal comments and opinion.

Review:

- Context—background information such as author, illustrator, artist, type of work, brief synopsis etc.
- Text description—describes elements of the text, artwork or production, such as the main characters and key incidents, stylistic features, staging
- Judgement—evaluation of the work by expressing an opinion or judgement.

Key grammatical features

- Use of particular nouns; factual and opinion adjectivals
- Relating verbs and action verbs in Context and Text Description stages; sensing verbs and relating verbs in Judgement stage
- Use of sensing verbs, Affect and Judgement vocabulary in the Description stage of a response
- Use of Appreciation vocabulary to evaluate aspects of text, artwork or performance in reviews.

Text A.14: Personal Response

Factory at Horta De Ebro

Context	The name of the painting is Factory at Horta De Ebro. It was painted by Pablo Picasso.
Opinion/ Reaction	I liked the painting but I think it was too gloomy and it made me feel sad and I wanted to cry. I like his other paintings a bit better than this one.

Text A.15: Review

Finding Nemo

Context

Finding Nemo is a children's fantasy movie produced in the popular animated style of the *Toy Story* and *Monsters Inc.* movies. The movie is set in the sea and is the story of a quest to find a lost fish, Nemo.

Text Description

The main characters are three fish, a young clown fish called Nemo, his father, Marlin and a blue fish with a very short memory called Dory. On Nemo's first day at school he gets caught by a pair of scuba divers. His father goes to find him and on his way meets Dory. Together they set out on a mission to find Nemo and encounter many sea creatures including Bruce, Anchor and Crush. But danger awaits them!

Judgement

Finding Nemo was an enjoyable, heartwarming movie. Although it was funny it also had a valuable message. That was that it is cruel to take animals out of their natural habitat. This theme is important for people of all ages to think about. The voices were great and the special effects made the fish and birds seem very realistic too. We highly recommend *Finding Nemo* to all ages.

Joint Construction Year 4

Answers

Exercise 2.1

Table 2.1

Questions / Text Segments	What is the social purpose of the text?	Is the segment taken from the beginning, middle or end of the text? How do you know?
Segment 1.1 OK, well turn on the oven first	To instruct someone how to do something.	Beginning—I know that when cooking you generally turn on the oven to start with so that it's at the right temperature.
Segment 1.2 In conclusion, bikes should only be ridden on the footpath.	To state a position with respect to an issue and argue a case for or against.	End. The words 'In conclusion' indicate that this is the end of the text.
Segment 1.3 Once upon a time …	To entertain and instruct through dealing with unusual and unexpected events.	Beginning. The phrase 'Once upon a time' traditional beginning for a fairy story.
Segment 1.4 After we visited the museum, we returned to school.	To retell a series of events in the sequence in which they occurred.	End. The word 'returned' indicates that it is the end of a series of events.
Segment 1.5 The tallest hardwood tree in the world is the mountain ash.	To classify and describe general classes of phenomena.	Beginning. This segment identifies and classifies the mountain ash in a general way so is probably at the beginning of the text.
Segment 1.6 This leads to soil erosion.	To explain how phenomena come into being.	Middle or End. The backwards reference word 'This' indicates that this is not the beginning of the text. There is no obvious concluding expression.

Exercise 2.2

Text 2.4

Social Purpose: To state a position with respect to an issue and argue a case for or against.
Text type: Exposition
Text Structure: Position; Arguments; Conclusion

Text 2.5

Social Purpose: To classify and describe general classes of phenomena.
Text Type: Information Report
Text Structure: General classification; Description (broad-leafed); Description (narrow-leafed)

Exercise 3.2

Carefully	place	spoonfuls of the mixture	onto a baking tray.
How	Action	What	Where

During his early career	Nikolai Poliakoff	experienced	many hardships.
When	Who	Action	What

Mum	found	a packet of cigarettes	in his bag.
Who	Action	What	Where

Exercise 3.3

Text 3.1

Social purpose: Retell events in the past.
Text type: Literary recount

On Tuesday	our class	visited	the aquarium.
Adverbial phrase	Noun group	Verb group	Noun group

We	saw	lots of sea creatures.
Pronoun	Verb group	Noun group

A shark with razor sharp teeth	was chasing	a school of small fish
Noun group	Verb group	Noun group

but	they	swam away	very quickly.
Conjunction	Pronoun	Verb group	Adverb

Then	some kids	fed	the dolphins.
Text connective	Noun group	Verb group	Noun group

At the end of the day	we	were allowed to buy	an ice cream.
Adverbial phrase	Pronoun	Verb group	Noun group

Text 3.2

Social purpose: To entertain through telling a story.
Probable text type: Narrative

Emma	was hiding	behind the door.
Noun group	Verb group	Adverbial phrase

After a while	she	peeked	into the room
Adverbial phrase	Pronoun	Verb group	Adverbial phrase

and	saw	a giant with huge bulging eyes.
Conjunction	Verb group	Noun group

He	was wearing	an old tattered coat
Pronoun	Verb group	Noun group

and	had	a black patch	over his left eye.
Conjunction	Verb group	Noun group	Adverbial phrase

When	the giant	walked	towards the door,
Conjunction	Noun group	Verb group	Adverbial phrase

Emma	took	a deep breath.
Noun group	Verb group	Noun group

Exercise 3.4 (example answers)

Mice	have	long tails.
ng	vg	ng

On the weekend	my mum	caught	three fish.
adv. p	ng	vg	ng

Put	the food colouring	in the beaker	slowly.
vg	ng	adv. p	adv.

Exercise 3.5

Clause	Clause type	Sentence type
When tobacco burns,	Dependent	Complex
it produces soot, tar, and nicotine.	Independent	
All of these are inhaled into the lungs.	Independent	Simple
Nicotine increases the heart rate and blood pressure	Independent	Compound
and gives smokers an enjoyable 'lift'.	Independent	
The other important substance in tobacco smoke is tar,	Independent	Complex
which leaves dark marks on the fingers and teeth of smokers.	Dependent	
Tar damages the lungs,	Independent	Complex
causing smokers cough.	Dependent	

Exercise 4.1

Type of verb group	Examples from Text 4.1
Action verb	arrived, are staying, snorkelled, took
Saying verb	called, said
Sensing verb	felt, loathe
Relating verb	has, are, have, were

Exercise 4.2

Noun group	Types
mosquitos	Living; non-human; general; everyday; concrete
insects	Living; non-human; general; everyday; concrete
a sucking tube	General; everyday; concrete
a proboscis	General; technical; concrete
larvae	General; technical; concrete
you	Living; human; particular
two itchy mosquito bites	Particular; everyday; concrete; subjective
my ankle	Living; human; particular; everyday; concrete

Exercise 4.3

Type of adverbial	Examples from Text 4.1
Place	in Cairns, in a small hotel, next to the marina, near the outer reef, near the pontoon
Time	on Sunday, Yesterday, Moments later
Manner	with his underwater camera

Exercise 4.4

Type of verb group	Examples from Text 4.3
Action verb	had been **driving**; having **modified**; could **sit**; began to **cross**; were being **swept away**
Saying verb	**shouted**
Sensing verb	had probably **frightened**; **watched**

Exercise 4.5

Text 4.4

the	spectacular	sight	of the fire
determiner	opinion adj.	noun	adj. phrase

some	news	that was frightening
determiner	noun	adj. clause

a	horrifying	thought
determiner	opinion adj.	noun

the	local	fire	brigade
determiner	classifier	classifier	noun

the	fierce	heat
determiner	opinion adj.	noun

this	dreadful	natural	disaster
determiner	opinion adj.	classifier	noun

Text 4.5

an	external	heat	source
determiner	classifier	classifier	noun

One	factor	which affects fire behaviour
Quantity adj.	noun	adj. clause

the	moisture	content	of the fuel
determiner	classifier	noun	adj. phrase

very	fine	fuels	like grasses
Intensifier	factual adj.	noun	adj. phrase

the	windspeed	at the firefront
determiner	noun	adj. phrase

an	important	consideration
determiner	opinion adj.	noun

Exercise 4.6

Type of adverbial	Text 4.6	Text 4.7
Place	in a bowl, onto a greased baking tray	In the middle of a dark forest, in an old tumble-down house, into the forest, in the distance, under a fallen log
Time		Once upon a time, one day, by nightfall
Extent	for 15 minutes	After two long hours
Manner	well, carefully, generously, with sifted icing sugar	
Accompaniment		with her father, her brother and three cats

The purpose of Text 4.6 is to provide a set of instructions (recipe) for someone to follow. The adverbials of place, manner and extent remind the reader of specific details that are important at particular steps. Adverbials are important in procedures because they help the reader to successfully accomplish the task at hand. The purpose of Text 4.7 is to entertain by telling a story. In narratives, adverbials are important resources for setting the scene, describing events and signalling a shift in stages.

Exercise 4.7

Text 4.8

Grammatical features	Examples
Generalised non-human participants	High pressure systems, masses of air, the cool air, stable weather conditions
Action verbs: present tense	Are **falling**, begin to **form**, not **heated**, **contracts**
Relating verbs linking causes and effects	Associated with, becomes, causes, produce
Factual and classifying adjectivals	**High pressure** systems; **stable weather** conditions; the **cool** air; **sunny, fine** days and **mild** nights
Technical terms	Pressure, surface
Nominalisation	Systems, conditions, increase

Text 4.9

Grammatical features	Examples
Action verbs	were driving, grew, fell, were trapped, lit up, hit, has been split, started, drove, gulped
Saying verbs	yelled, whispered
Sensing verbs	looked, knew, heard, were terrified, realised, stared
Particular human and non-human participants	Jack, the show, the window, a storm, a huge gum tree, the road, another bolt, the tree trunk, the car, the tall figure
Opinion adjectivals	spectacular, eerie, mysterious
Factual adjectivals	dark, huge, ear-splitting, shattered, tall
Adverbials	One dark night, to the show, in the distance, behind us, a few seconds later, across the road, in front of us, in half, through the gap between the shattered branches

Exercise 4.8

This report about spiders contains a General Classification stage identifying different ways that spiders can be classified. The second paragraph gives a description of appearance, habitat and how they catch prey. The student uses relating verbs to classify spiders and describe their appearance (eg. *are, belong to, have*) and action verbs to describe behaviour (eg. *live, eat, lie, grab, inject, bite*). The noun groups are generalised and objective and include classifiers (eg. *the* **arachnid** *family,* **trapdoor** *spiders*) and factual adjectivals to build up descriptions (eg. *a* **light brown** *body and a* **grey** *cephalothorax,* **big** *insects like moths and grasshoppers*). The adverbials of place, *in a burrow* and *at the top of the burrow*, add detail to the description.

Exercise 4.9

Text 4.11

The Zoo

Last week our class went to the zoo. We arrived at school very early to catch the bus. We saw lots of different animals and had a picnic lunch. I am going to tell you about the snakes in the reptile house. There were lots of awesome species of snakes. Snakes bodies are long and thin and covered with scales. One snake was eating a dead rat. It looked really gross. Then we saw a huge python. Did you know that some snakes use venom and others strangle their prey? Jack wants a pet snake for Christmas but luckily his mum won't let him.

The expectation was probably for the students to write a recount, however the teacher was not clear about the purpose for writing. This text has no clear focus and the student mixes recount with some description as well as personal comment. As a result it is not a successful text. This is reflected in the mixture of verb groups—action and sensing for telling about events and feelings, and relating for descriptions of animals. Also, some verbs are in the past tense and others are in the present as the writer switches back and forth between the past and the here and now. The noun groups are mostly simple, naming a variety of particular people or things (eg. *our class, we, the bus, a huge python, Jack*) as well as 'snakes' in a generalised way. There are a few factual adjectivals (eg. *long, thing*) and classifiers (eg. **picnic** *lunch,* **pet** *snake*). Because so much of the text reflects personal opinion and attitude there are also opinion adjectivals (eg. *awesome, gross, huge*).

To write a recount, the student would need to focus on retelling a sequence of important or interesting events and leave out clauses that related to other purposes. This may include better use of adverbials of time and place. To write an information report, the student would first need to choose a topic for their description. This might be a description of some of the features of the zoo they visited, a report about 'zoos' in general or a report describing the features of some of the animals they saw. The descriptions would need to be clustered into 'groups' of related information such as appearance, habitat, behaviour, diet etc. The student would need to focus on the use of relating and action verbs, as well as factual adjectivals and classifiers in the noun groups.

Exercise 5.1

Text 5.1 would be found at the beginning of an interactive CD ROM or web-site. It could also come from a children's book about the sea if the instruction 'Click me' was changed to 'Turn the page!'. The text is trying to motivate users to find out more information about sea creatures. More broadly, it is trying to entertain and give information.

Exercise 5.2

Clause	Type of clause	Way of interacting
Have you ever wondered about the sea?	Question (Rhetorical; Yes/No)	To encourage someone to think about something
No there's not!	Exclamation	To express disagreement in an emphatic way
The sea is certainly fascinating and mysterious.	Statement	To give information
Want to come on a sea voyage with me?	Question (Yes/No)	To make an offer
Click me!	Command	To get something done

Exercise 5.3

Clauses from Text 5.2	Type of clause	Way of interacting
So, what can you see in the picture?	Question (Open Wh-)	To ask for information
There are some kids at the skateboard park?	Statement (with rising intonation)	To give information tentatively
That big kid standing up is smoking Miss.	Statement	To give information
Yes Penny, but could you put your hand up next time?	Question	To ask someone to do something
And Jenny, leave Rosie alone.	Command	To get something done directly
Does your brother smoke at home?	Question (Closed; Yes/No)	Asking for information

This is typical of much classroom interaction. The teacher is in control of the interaction, initiating discussion and eliciting information (that she presumably already knows) from students and moving on to ask for information she doesn't know. She uses a mixture of open and closed questions to get information. The teacher in involved in both teaching content and regulating behaviour. The teacher uses indirect and direct ways of managing the classroom. She gets students to do things by direct commands and by asking questions that function indirectly as a command (eg. *Could you put your hand up next time?*).

The teacher is more powerful than the students. For example, the teacher initiates the discussion with questions, she uses commands and she can talk to them without putting her hand up. The students and teacher know each other well, but there is a difference in status. For example, the teacher knows and uses students' first names but they call her 'Miss'. The students seem to feel relatively comfortable with the teacher. For example, Penny interrupts and is not deterred from continuing to add to the discussion after the teacher has indirectly reprimanded her. Penny also speaks of personal topics and uses everyday colloquial language (eg. *grounded*), which is often associated with a greater degree of affective involvement among the participants.

Exercise 5.4

The main type of modality expressed in Text 5.5 is probability (*could, may, might, perhaps*).

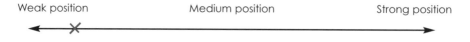

Weak position   Medium position   Strong position

The main type of modality expressed in Text 5.6 is obligation (*must, had to*).

Weak position   Medium position   Strong position

Exercise 5.5

Expression from Text 5.5	Type of modality	Degree of modality	Grammatical structure
possible	probability	low	Modal adjectival
Perhaps	probability	low	Modal adverbial
might	probability	low	Modal verb
may	probability	low	Modal verb
could	probability	low	Modal verb
possibly	probability	low	Modal adverbial
need	obligation	high	Modal verb

Expression from Text 5.6	Type of modality	Degree of modality	Grammatical structure
I believe	probability	high	Modal clause
must	obligation	high	Modal verb
had to	obligation	high	Modal verb
would	probability	medium	Modal verb
have to	obligation	high	Modal verb
need	obligation	high	Modal verb

Exercise 5.6

Text 5.8 (examples)

'Please fasten your seatbelts for take-off!'
This was it! Take-off! That dreaded word! The last of Amy's confidence evaporated and a wave of fear swept over her. Oh how she hated take-off! She fumbled nervously with the clasp of her seatbelt and then she grasped her father's hand as the great white plane moved slowly along the runway. Her father pressed her hand reassuringly but Amy was too frightened to look up at him. The plane picked up speed and the fear rose to pure terror in Amy's stomach. She stole an anxious glance around her—Gilly was grinning delightedly as she pointed out landmarks to an equally excited Andrew. How could they be so happy! Her mother, too, seemed relaxed and confident as she gazed calmly out over the water and her father... why, was that a nervous tick she detected on her father's cheek as he studiously studied the inflight magazine? Amy was momentarily distracted as she contemplated her anxious father staring unseeingly at the page, his hand growing ever tighter around Amy's on the arm of the seat. But then as the plane lurched into the air, her own fear returned with full force and the insides of her stomach churned like butter. Up! Up! Oh when would it stop? Her fingernails dug into her father's hand as the plane continued it's ascent—higher, higher... and then
'Ladies and Gentlemen, Boys and Girls! You may now unfasten your seatbelts and move around the cabin...'
It was over! The realisation hit her with a bolt—the anxiety vanished and she looked up excitedly. Her father looked at her a little sheepishly. Then they both laughed with relief.
'Whoopee!' Amy cried joyously, 'Currumbin Beach, here we come!'

Character	Feeling/s		
	Beginning	Middle	End
Amy	afraid	terrified	relieved and happy
Father	calm	nervous	a little embarrassed, relieved and happy
Gilly	not known	excited and happy	not known
Andrew	not known	excited and happy	not known
Mother	not known	relaxed and confident	not known

Exercise 5.7

Emotional Categories	Expressions from Text 5.8
Happiness	grinning, joyously, laughed, excited
Unhappiness	hated, dreaded
Security	calmly, relaxed, confident, relief
Insecurity	frightened, nervously, anxious, terror
Satisfaction	—
Dissatisfaction	sheepishly

Exercise 5.8

Indirect Expression of Affect	Emotional category
she grasped her father's hand	Insecurity
stole an anxious glance	insecurity
She pointed out landmarks	Security, happiness
She gazed calmly out over the water	Security
He studiously studied the inflight magazine	Insecurity
(her father)... staring unseeingly at the page, his hand growing ever tighter around Amy's on the arm of the seat.	Insecurity
the insides of her stomach churned like butter.	Insecurity
Oh when would it stop?	Insecurity
Her fingernails dug into her father's hand	Insecurity
'Whoopee!'	Happiness
'Currumbin Beach, here we come!'	Happiness

Exercise 5.9

The purpose of Text 5.9 is to give information, to give instructions for action. The evaluations are mainly positive at the beginning of the text when it is outlining expected behaviour and mainly negative when it is 'giving permission' for people to rebel. The purpose of Text 5.10 is to retell the events of a person's life (biographical recount). We would probably find Text 5.10 in a textbook or historical document in a museum. The behaviour of the British people is evaluated as warmongering, immoral and lacking in courage.

Exercise 5.10

Text 5.9 (Indirect expressions italicised)

Person, group or institution who is judged	Main type/s of Judgement used	Positive or Negative	Examples
People	Social Sanction	Positive	Kindly, tolerantly, fairly, justly, without discrimination, *may be necessary to rebel (ie. rebellious)*
Regimes	Social Sanction	Negative	Corrupt, cruel, tyranny, oppression, *regimes have resulted in barbarous and evil acts*

Text 5.10 (Indirect expressions italicised)

Person, group or institution who is judged	Main type/s of Judgement used	Positive or Negative	Examples
Pemulwuy	Social Esteem	Positive	Brave, famous, effective, *so strong that he managed to escape from his chains; led the people in guerrilla war against the invaders; organised many attacks ...; managed to escape; ability to escape capture and survive;* important, historical
	Social Sanction	Positive	*... against the invaders; ... against the British who had invaded and occupied sacred land; encouraged his people to defend their land and free themselves from white invaders*
British soldiers	Social Esteem	Negative	Afraid; *they believed he was magic*
British	Social Sanction	Negative	Invaders; *invaded and occupied sacred land*

Exercise 5.11

Text 5.11 is a description. The descriptions are mainly adjectivals which describe the specialness of the place, in terms of physical beauty and remoteness. Text 5.12 is a review. The type of descriptions are adjectivals as well as phrases and whole clauses. The writer is assessing the book mainly in terms of how the text is constructed and whether or not it is a worthwhile book in terms of culturally valued themes (eg. friendship).

Exercise 5.12

Text 5.11 Expressions of Appreciation

Category	Positive	Negative
Reaction	Wonderful, peaceful, beautiful, tropical, bright, colourful, vivid, special, rare, delicate	noisy, busy

Text 5.12 Expressions of Appreciation

Category	Positive	Negative
Reaction	a bushy feeling, beautiful, interesting	
Composition	Effective, sophisticated, matches with the outback pictures, work together for the exact effect that the writer and illustrator wanted.	Quick, rough, like a draft
Valuation	Interesting, a story of a friendship, meaningful, suitable, the story reminds us of traditional European fables.	

Text 5.11 uses mainly reaction expressions because it is trying to build up a picture of the garden for the reader to share. Text 5.12 uses mainly composition and valuation expressions because it focuses on assessing the way the book was written and the value or worth of the book. While 'interesting' could be coded as an expression of Affect, there is also an argument for coding it as valuation. Note that although this Text 5.12 does include negative expressions, they are made positive by the use of the words 'but' and 'seems'.

Note also that some expressions may be used to assess both the emotional reaction and the worth of the book (eg. *interesting; the story reminds us of traditional European fables*).

Exercise 5.13

The texts share the same basic purpose of retelling a series of events for the purpose of entertaining, however the words and phrases highlighted make the events in Text 5.14 seem more dramatic.

Text 5. 14

One stormy night I woke up busting to go to the toilet. It was pitch dark and I was so scared my teeth were chattering. I slowly, slowly crept down the endless hall and then Squelch! Something horribly slimey oozed through my toes. I let out an ear piercing scream and Mum came hurtling out of her bedroom looking like a ghost. She snapped the light switch to reveal runny cat poo all over my foot! It was so gross!

Exercise 5.14

Interpersonal resources	Examples from Text 5.16
Modality to express degrees of probability, usuality, obligation and inclination	couldn't
Comment adverbials to give the speaker or writer's opinion	Unfortunately
Affect vocabulary to express the feelings of the people involved	couldn't wait, enjoy
Judgement vocabulary to evaluate people's behaviour	creative, famous, carefully, skilfully, fussy, angry, sneak, attentively, never managed, not patient
Appreciation vocabulary to describe scenes and describe what things look like	favourite, perfectly formed, magical, sweet, crunchy, melt in your mouth, wonderful, towering with mile-high golden
Direct and indirect grading expressions to make evaluations more intense or less intense.	very, especially, quite, perfectly, towering, mile-high, never, just

Exercise 5.15

Interpersonal resources	Examples from Text 5.17
Statements to build an impersonal and objective relationship with the reader or listener	In recent years there has been a great deal of debate over whether rainforests should be logged.
Modality to express degrees of probability, usuality and obligation	The logging industry thinks that, necessary, conservationists believe that, need, should, will, could, in some cases, already, it is clear that
Judgement vocabulary to evaluate the behaviour of groups of people	protected, creates many jobs, supports the economy, will lose their jobs, phase out logging gradually, develop eco-tourism, provide employment
Appreciation vocabulary to assess significance and importance	employment, the economy, valuable, significant social upheaval, death, important, placing the delicate rainforest ecosystem at risk, destroying, irreplaceable, kill many animals, destroying their habitats, not simple, employment, environment, priceless, sustainable
Direct and indirect grading expressions to make evaluations more intense or less intense.	very, extremely

Note that many expressions which seem to be Judgements are actually expressed as expressions of Appreciation: valuation in this text because it is not a person, group or institution whose actions are evaluated (eg. in paragraph 2, the negative effects of logging are not attributed to the logging workers or even the industry). This is a result of nominalisation and is a way of removing human agency from texts. See Chapter 7 for more discussion.

Exercise 5.16

The writer is trying to persuade the reader against taking some action (not to kill spiders). The child has begun with a statement of opinion (thesis) and then given a series of arguments in the form of reasons (kill flies and mosquitos, make nice webs, do not hurt anyone) and ended with an emotional appeal to the reader which reinforces the thesis. The child has used statements, rhetorical questions and commands to interact with the reader. The statements provide information which support the thesis—however, the questions and commands take the focus off providing the information and could be confronting to the reader.

Impersonal   Personal

Formal   Informal

It could be suggested that the student use statements which will be able to give the reader more information about the worth of spiders and the consequences of killing them. Using commands may make the writer feel like they were being given an order.

Exercise 5.17

The writer has used very high modality which could put the reader off side. The writer has used a command to get the reader to act. This could also be too confronting in this situation and not get the results the writer wants.

Clauses from Text 5.19	Tempered version (example)
I am **completely unable** to hear my television.	**It is often difficult** for me to hear my television.
The dog also keeps me awake **every night**.	The dog **often** keeps me awake
I **must** have my sleep,	**Unfortunately**, I am unable to do without sleep
Please keep your dog quiet. (command) please (question)	**Would you mind** trying to keep your dog quiet
Either lock it inside the house or in the garage. (command)	**Perhaps** you **could** lock it inside the house or in the garage. (statement)

Exercise 6.1

Text 6.1 is an exposition. Its purpose is to persuade the reader by stating a position and supporting that with a series of arguments. The writer helps the reader make an initial prediction about the way in which the whole text will develop by using the words many reasons. This sets up an expectation that these 'reasons' will be outlined. The content of the following paragraphs is signalled by the first sentence of each paragraph. These sentences help organise the writer's argument by naming each of the reasons for banning bikes in national parks.

Exercise 6.2

Text 6.2

Many species of animals are threatened with extinction because of the way people change the land. The main threats to animals are loss of habitat, introduced animals and hunting.

Loss of habitat

Loss of habitat has already led to the extinction of many species of animals. When people clear land for housing and roads, there is no longer enough space and food for the animals living in the area. This kind of development also increases the amount of pollution which harms animals and their habitats.

Introduced animals

Introduced animals are those that are brought to an area where they do not naturally live. Many introduced animals, such as cats, foxes and rabbits, threaten the survival of native animals. For example, in Australia, foxes and cats hunt native animals, and rabbits eat the plants the native animals feed on.

Hunting

Many animals are hunted by people. Some are killed for their meat, fur and body parts. Others are hunted for sport or for trophies and souvenirs. Some of the biggest animals in the world, such as whales and elephants, have almost been hunted to extinction.

Text 6.2 is a report describing the main threats to animals. Headings and sub-headings often function in the same way as text and paragraph previews, particularly in information books for young readers. In reports such as this, headings help with the topical organisation of information. The order of the points in a text preview should be followed in the body of the text. Similarly, all points in the text preview should be addressed in the body and the body should not introduce any points that have not first been introduced in the text preview. This ensures the readers' expectations are met and helps make the text coherent.

Exercise 6.3

Rewritten text (example only):

There are four main types of clowns. They are Whiteface clowns, Auguste clowns, Character clowns and New Vaudeville clowns.

Whiteface clowns evolved from the theatrical entertainers of earlier times. These clowns cover their face with white make-up and do a lot of physical stunts like leaping and tumbling.

Auguste clowns became popular during the nineteenth century. Auguste clowns wear colourful, ill fitting clothing and oversized shoes. They also have bulbous noses and brightly coloured wigs.

Another type of clown is the Character clown. These clowns make fun of the human condition and may impersonate characters such as a cowboy, fireman, tramp or policeman.

"New Vaudeville" clowns are a more recent type of clown. They involve the audience in the performance. Their act may consist of mime, juggling, acrobatics, magic tricks and traditional clowning.

Exercise 6.5

Text 6.4

Dawn Fraser is an Australian swimming legend. She was born in 1937 in Balmain, Sydney. As a young child, Dawn had asthma and began swimming because it helped her breathing. During her teens, she trained with coach Harry Gallagher and in 1956 qualified for the Melbourne Olympics, where she won her first gold medal. After that, Dawn became a permanent member of the Australian Swimming Team. In 1962, Dawn became the first woman to swim 100 metres in less than a minute. After the Tokyo Olympics in 1964, Dawn was banned from competition for ten years for something she didn't do. This caused her early retirement from swimming. Since then she has become a celebrity, running a pub in Balmain and more recently, taking an active role in politics.

Source: http://www.abc.net.au/btn/australians/fraser.htm

Text 6.5

Kangaroos are Australia's largest marsupial. Their scientific name is Macropus rufus. Kangaroos live in open forests and grasslands. They like to shelter from the sun under shady trees. Kangaroos have 2 small front feet which are like hands. They use these to scratch themselves and hold food. They have much bigger hind legs for hopping. Some kangaroos can leap 8 metres in a single bound. Kangaroos can move as fast as 40-50 km per hour.

Exercise 6.6

Fill a jar half full with water. (verb)
Pour some cooking oil on top. (verb)
Put the lid on (verb)
and **shake**. (verb)
After a few minutes, the oil floats back to the top. (adverbial)
Oil is a liquid that won't dissolve in water. (noun group)
Water is also heavier (noun group)
and **it** sinks to the bottom. (pronoun)

Exercise 6.7

Text 6. 6

Make a decorative jar of stones

Firstly, collect some stones with interesting shapes, textures and colours.

Put them in a bowl of warm soapy water

and scrub them with a brush.

Then rinse the stones

and stand them on a window sill for a day.

Next, give the stones a thin coat of varnish.

Let the varnish dry.

Finally, arrange the stones in a glass jar or container

and use it as an ornament.

The purpose of Text 6.6 (a procedure) is to provide a series of instructions for making something. Textual themes are often used in procedures to give an order or sequence to the steps that need to be followed. The experiential themes of each clause are action verbs specifying the 'task' that needs to be carried out at each step.

Exercise 6.11

Grammatical features of Text 6.7	Examples
Complex and compound sentences	When people clear land for houses and roads they change the environment.
	Forest and bushland is destroyed and many animals lose their homes.
	Some animals have become extinct because their homes have been destroyed.
Simple noun groups (or pronouns) about people, concrete things	People, they, forest and bushland, many animals, their homes, more houses and roads
Clauses with action verbs and human 'actors'	When people clear land, they change the environment.
	They destroy the forest and bushland. More houses and roads will pollute the environment.
Conjunctions expressing cause/effect between clauses	When, and then, because

Grammatical features of Text 6.8	Examples
Simple sentences	It may also increase the level of pollution. Loss of habitat has already led to the extinction of many species of animals.
Longer noun groups about abstract things	the extinction of many species of animals; the destruction of the natural habitat of many local species
Clauses with relating verbs expressing cause/effect— no human 'actors'	often results in, may increase, has led to

Exercise 6.12 (suggested answers only)

i. There has been recent global debate concerning the possibility of an increase in the hole in the ozone layer.
ii. An increase in urbanisation may result in higher levels of pollution and inadequate housing.

Exercise 6.13

Nominalisations: killing, issue, decline, extinction.
(An example using five clauses instead of two) Marine biologists are worried because so many sharks are being killed unnecessarily. If too many sharks are killed their numbers will start to get low and some species of sharks might become extinct.

Exercise 6.14

The oesophagus lies beneath the trachea inside the chest. It runs behind the lungs and heart. This is the view down the inside of the oesophagus. Beneath its mucus-covered lining there are muscles that run down the length of the oesophagus and in a circular pattern around it. These muscles take over from the throat muscles after food is swallowed. They work together to squeeze the softened food down towards the stomach. This is the next stop on our journey.

Source: *The Human Body* (Harris 2000:11)

Exercise 6.15

Type of lexical cohesion	Examples from Text 6.13
The use of **synonyms** ie. words that are similar in meaning.	Junk food/unhealthy food; packets/wrappers
The use of **antonyms** ie. words that have opposite or contrastive meanings.	Unhealthy food/healthy foods
The use of **repetition** ie. words that are repeated across a text.	Junk food
The use of **collocation** ie. words that co-occur because they share a common element of meaning.	School canteen/rubbish/playground/students
Words that form a **class/sub-class** relationship.	•Junk food: chocolate bars/ice-creams/coke/sweets •Chemicals/food colouring
Words that form a **whole/part** relationship.	School: canteen/playground Junk food: sugar/fat/food colouring/chemicals

Exercise 6.16

The purpose of Text 6.14 is to describe some of the features of cities. It is an information report written by an older student, organised into paragraphs. The Classification stage contains a text preview naming the features that will be described ie. buildings, population, landmarks and social problems. Each point is described in a separate paragraph, signalled by a paragraph preview. The student uses themes that repeat some kind of reference to the topic and makes use of the zig-zag pattern in some paragraphs.

Nominalisation: a large population, the population of Sydney, social problems, unemployment, homelessness, popular tourist attractions
Text connectives:
Clarifying: For example, For instance
Sequencing ideas: Firstly
Adding information: In addition, also

Class/sub-class	Social problems: unemployment, homelessness, drugs, street gangs Modern buildings: Centrepoint Tower, Opera House Old buildings: Queen Victoria Building, Hyde Park Barracks Man-made landmarks: Taronga Park Zoo, Harbour Bridge, Darling Harbour Natural landmarks: Bondi Beach, Great Barrier Reef, Kakadu National Park
Whole/part	Population: people from Vietnam, Greece, Lebanon, Japan, Samoa, Yugoslavia
Synonyms	Cities/towns; tourist attractions/landmarks
Antonyms	Modern (buildings)/old (buildings); Man-made landmarks/natural landmarks
Repetition	Cities
Collocation	Cities/buildings/people

Exercise 6.17

Text 6.15

Brachiosaurus was a reptile. He had a long tail and a long neck. He walked on four legs. He was a herbivore and it ate plants. He lived in water. They laid more than one egg.

This text has a problem with reference. The reference pronoun *he* should only be used when the gender is known. Pronouns referring back to *Brachiosaurus* are also used inconsistently ie. *he, it* (singular) and *they* (plural). The writer uses a compound sentence to combine information.

Text 6.16

Brontosaurus was a reptile. Brontosaurus was 20 metres long. Brontosaurus walked on 4 legs. Brontosaurus was a herbivore. Brontosaurus lived on land.

To avoid this repetition, the student could replace some instances of Brontosaurus with the reference pronoun 'it'. The student could also combine some of the simple sentences into compound sentences. Both these strategies would make the text more cohesive.

Text 6.17

On Friday our class walked to Blackstump Creek to study the water environment. Our group had to record the different types of plants. First we looked at the water plants. We waded into the water to see what plants were growing in the shallow parts. Then we recorded it on the sheet of paper. Then we looked at the plants growing on the banks and then we had to sketch some of them. Then it was time to go back to school. Then we recorded our information on the computer.

The purpose of Text 6.17, a procedural recount, is to retell the procedures followed on a class field trip. The textual themes are nearly all the text connective *then* (except for the first time adverbial). The experiential themes focus on the 'doers' of all the actions ie. *we/our group*. To avoid the endless repetition of *then*, the student could use a wider variety of time adverbials and text connectives indicating time.

References

Australian Broadcasting Corporation (Online 2003 November 7) <http://www.abc.net.au/btn/australians/fraser.htm>

Board of Studies NSW (1998) English K-6 Syllabus, Sydney: New South Wales Department of Education and Training, <http://www.bosnsw-k6.nsw.edu.au>

Board of Studies NSW (1998) English K-6 Modules, Sydney: New South Wales Department of Education and Training, <http://www.bosnsw-k6.nsw.edu.au>

Board of Studies NSW, 'State and Federal Government', Stage 3 Units for Human Society and Its Environment K-6, Sydney: New South Wales Department of Education and Training.

Bookweek-Picture Books rap (2001). Professional Support and Curriculum, Sydney: New South Wales Department of Education and Training.

Bruner J.S (1978) 'The Role of Dialogue in Language Acquisition' In Sinclair, A., Jarvella, R. & Levelt, W. (eds.) The Child's Conception of Language, New York: Springer-Verlag.

Callaghan, M. & Rothery, J. (1988) Teaching Factual Writing: A Genre-Based Approach, Metropolitan East Disadvantaged Schools Program, Erskineville.

COBUILD (1990) English Grammar, London: HarperCollins.

Coffin, C. (1996) Exploring Literacy in School History, Sydney: NSW Department of School Education.

Collerson, J. (1994) English Grammar: A Functional Approach, Sydney: Primary English Teaching Association.

Collerson, J. (1997) Grammar in Teaching, Sydney: Primary English Teaching Association.

Dahl, R. (1982) The BFG, Victoria: Puffin Books.

Derewianka, B. (1998) A Grammar Companion for Primary Teachers, Sydney: Primary English Teaching Association.

Droga, L. & Humphrey, S. (2002) Getting Started with Functional Grammar, Berry: Target Texts.

Halliday, M.A.K. (1994) An Introduction to Functional Grammar, London: Edward Arnold.

Halliday, M.A.K. & Hasan, R. (1976) Cohesion in English, London: Longman.

Harris, N. (2000) The Human Body, Victoria: The Five Mile Press.

Howes, J. (1994) Wildlife at Risk, Melbourne: Macmillan Education Australia.

Humphrey, S. (1996) *Exploring Literacy in School Geography*, Sydney: NSW Department of School Education.

Klein, R. (1987) *Robin Klein's Crookbook*, North Ryde: Methuen.

Macken-Horarik, M. (1996) 'Literacy and learning across the curriculum: towards a model of register for secondary school teachers', In Hasan, R. & Williams, G. (eds.), *Literacy in Society*, London: Longman. 232-78.

Martin, J.R. (1993) 'Genre and literacy–modelling context in educational linguistics', *Annual Review of Applied Linguistics*, 13: 141-72.

Martin, J.R. (1999) 'Mentoring semogenesis: genre-based literacy pedagogy revisited' In Christie, F. (ed.) *Pedagogy and the shaping of consciousness: linguistic and social processes*, London: Cassell. 123-55.

Martin, J.R. (2000a) 'Close reading: functional linguistics as a tool for critical discourse analysis' In Unsworth, L. (ed.) *Researching Language in schools and communities*, London: Cassell. 275-304.

Martin, J.R. (2000b) 'Beyond Exchange: APPRAISAL Systems in English' In Hunston, S. & Thompson, G. (eds.) *Evaluation in Text: Authorial Stance and the Construction of Discourse*, Oxford: Oxford University Press.

Martin, J.R. & Rose, D. (2003) *Working with Discourse; Meaning beyond the clause*, London: Continuum.

Rothery, R. (1994) *Exploring Literacy in School English*, Sydney: NSW Department of School Education.

Swortzell, L. (1978) *Here come the clowns*, New York: Viking Press.

Recommended reading

Building Understandings in Literacy and Teaching (BUILT), (2002) (2nd Edition). Love, K., Pigdon, K., Baker, G. & Hamston, J., CD ROM resource, The University of Melbourne, Melbourne University Publishing. <http://www.mup.unimelb.edu.au/e-showcase>

Butt, D., Fahey, R., Feez, S., Spinks, S., Yallop, C. (2000) *Using Functional Grammar: An Explorer's Guide*, Sydney: National Centre for English Language Teaching and Research, Macquarie University.

Christie, F. (ed.) (1990) *Literacy for a Changing World*, Hawthorn: Australian Council for Educational Research.

Curriculum Corporation (1994) *A Statement on English for Australian Schools*, (a joint project of the States, Territories and the Commonwealth of Australia initiated by the Australian Education Council), Melbourne: Curriculum Corporation.

Derewianka, B. (1991) *Exploring How Texts Work*, Sydney: Primary English Teaching Association.

Derewianka, B. (ed.) (1992) *Language Assessment in Primary Classrooms*, Marrickville: Harcourt Brace Jovanovich.

Feez, S. & Joyce, H. (1998) *Writing Skills: Narrative & Non-Fiction Text Types*, Albert Park, Australia: Phoenix Education.

Gibbons, P. (2002) *Scaffolding language, scaffolding learning: teaching second language learners in the mainstream classroom,* Portsmouth, NH: Heinemann.

Hammond, J. (ed.) (2001) *Scaffolding: teaching and learning in language and literacy education*, Sydney: Primary English Teaching Association.

Jones, P. (ed.) (1996) *Talking to Learn*, Sydney: Primary English Teaching Association.

Martin, J.R. (1997) 'Analysing Genre: Functional Parameters' In Christie, F. & Martin, J.R. (eds.) *Genre and Institutions: Social Processes in the Workplace and School*, London: Cassell.

Painter, C. (2001) 'Understanding Genre and Register: Implications for Language Teaching' In Burns, A. & Coffin, C. (eds.), *Analysing English in a Global Context*, London: Routledge.

Priority Schools Funding Program (2002) Reading Texts in Stages 3 and 4: Science, History and Geography. CD ROM Database of text types, Sydney: NSW Department of Education and Training.

Unsworth, L. (ed.) (2000) *Researching Language in schools and communities*, London: Cassell.

Unsworth, L. (2001) *Teaching multiliteracies across the curriculum: Changing contexts of text and image in classroom practice*, Buckingham: Open University Press.

Vygotsky, L.S. (1962) *Thought and Language*, Cambridge, MA: MIT Press.